Old
is not a
four-letter word

A GUIDEBOOK FOR THE JOURNEY THROUGH OLD

Old
is not a
four-letter word

A GUIDEBOOK FOR THE JOURNEY THROUGH OLD

Susan M. Towle, RN

Old Is Not a Four-Letter Word: A Guidebook for the Journey through Old

ISBN: 978-1503346017

EDITORIAL CONSULTANTS: JOHN BUDZ, VEE SAWYER & ASHLEY GRAHAM
BOOK PRODUCTION: WARD STREET PRESS
DESIGN BY VEE SAWYER

To my beloved children, Jennifer and Andrew,
who continue to be the wind beneath my wings.

May your aging journey be filled with health, joy, and grace.

■　■　■

CONTENTS

CHAPTER FOUR
MEDICAL CARE AND MEDICATIONS

CHAPTER FIVE
QUALITY OF LIFE

CHAPTER SIX
SOCIALIZATION

Old
is not a
four-letter word

A GUIDEBOOK FOR THE JOURNEY THROUGH OLD

PROLOGUE

The purpose of this guidebook has grown out of my four decades as a Registered Nurse (RN) with many years spent in elder care. I have become impassioned about turning the tide regarding our lack of preparedness for our physical, mental, emotional, and spiritual wellbeing during the years that most of us will spend on what I see as the *Journey through Old*. We act as though we are deer caught in the lights when we have any kind of glitch in the road or crisis on that journey. This *Journey through Old* is guaranteed to have some glitches and potential crises, and we need to be prepared.

The book addresses two audiences — the mentally cognizant elder and the adult child or caregiver of an elder. In my experience, never has a generation seemed so unprepared to face the inevitable changes that happen to us all, as we become old. In our youth-oriented culture, we try every anti-aging remedy that comes on the market in an effort to appear and act young, as though these efforts will somehow delay the inevitable. That denial of our natural aging makes for a very rough journey for a great number of us. Can we change that mindset? How did we get here in the first place? How do we become better prepared? This guidebook attempts to answer some of these questions and hopefully if you read and follow the suggestions, you will feel more confident and eager to embrace this unique and special time in your life — the *Journey through Old*. First, let's start with some aging stories that may indicate how we got here.

STORY: A FABLE BY TOLSTOY

 A young prince in a distant land was riding out into his realm for the first time with his wizard. He comes upon a man who is very wrinkled and bent over walking slowly along the path. "What is that?" asks the young prince. The wizard replied, "That is old. It is what happens when a person has lived for many years." The prince was astounded and immediately wheeled his horse around and headed quickly back to the castle not wanting to see such a thing ever again.

It was many months later when the wizard convinced the prince that he really had to leave the castle more often to experience more of the world. Once again, as they rode down a wooded path, they came to a group of people carrying a large wooden box and crying softly. "What is going on and what is in that box?" whispered the prince to the wizard. The wizard turned to the prince and said, "That is death. It is what happens to all of us eventually." Again the prince was shocked and quickly turned his horse around back to the castle.

Tolstoy was so immersed in what happens as age and eventually death overtake the body that he went into a deep depression for a period of time. Tolstoy asked the question, "What is the point of life if this is what happens?"[1]

STORY: NO PRINCES OR WIZARDS

 As a registered nurse elder care manager, I was called out to a house one day to talk with two adult children who seemed to be at their wits end with what to do about their parents, both in their mid-nineties. I usually tried to find out about the issues before visiting a family, but in this case, the daughter was too upset to talk and wanted her brother to be present as well.

The daughter met me at the door and invited me in, but would not talk with me about why she had called for my services until her brother returned home. I suggested we sit at the dining room table, and she nervously agreed. The brother was out with his father doing some errands. As the brother and his dad walked into the house, the brother clearly was frustrated and angry. His sister introduced us but instead of sitting at the table, he paced back and forth saying, "I'd like someone to explain to me what the fuck is going on here! Just what the fuck is happening here?" At first I did not know what he meant, so I asked if he could tell me why he was so upset. "Upset!" he said, "Upset! I'll tell you why I am upset! Something is going on here! I come over almost daily, clean this house, fill their mediplanner, try to help them all I can in addition to my full-time job and family. Every time I come over, the place is a mess even though I have told them a thousand times what to do. I have instructed my dad over and over about mom's mediplanner, and I find half the medications on the kitchen floor. He cannot seem to get even that straight. My dad is a smart man. He insists he can take care of things, but I am tired of this crap!" As he ranted and paced, he started to slow down, his head dropped, his shoulders drooped, and he eventually sat down in despair.

We sat in silence for a few seconds with the sister clearly anxious and fidgeting. I finally said, "It appears that you care very much for your parents, but what you are doing is not working." He looked at me fatigued and with tears forming in his eyes, he said, "You can say that again. Could someone just tell me what is going on?"

"It is called old," I replied. "Your parents are old, and at this point in their lives, they need help in ways which you are unable to give. By that I mean it will take much more than you dropping in every day or every other day. Your father has no memory; your mother continues to fall frequently; they clearly cannot manage this home, which is much too big for them at this point. You are also trying to teach them what to do when they are not teachable due to short-term memory loss. You cannot teach someone anything if they cannot remember. The reason you are so frustrated and angry is you are doing the same thing over and over and each time expecting the outcome to be different. Your parents cannot help the fact that their memory, hearing, sight, and abilities are declining. They are not behaving this way to make your life difficult."

"Well, deliver me. In that case, I want no part of this old business," the brother replied, sounding like the prince speaking in the Tolstoy story. I told him I understood his frustration, and now that he knew what was really happening, maybe we could look at some solutions. "Fine!" he said. "Now what is the solution going to cost?"

Unfortunately, the solution does cost, and for the most part, it can cost a lot, especially if no one has planned for the events and costs of old. As for the end of this story, the brother and sister were shocked at the cost of the solution, which was to hire a caregiver in the home on a daily basis for eight hours a day with registered nurse oversight. They were outraged by the cost, and they felt the government should be blamed for somehow not covering this cost in some way. (Medicare does not cover this kind of care.)

STORY: THE OLD AMONG US

 I was heading to the gym one early morning to join a yoga class. It was a large class, and we had to carefully space ourselves so as to accommodate everyone. One woman walked in just as the class was beginning and looked for some space. The sweet, youthful instructor at the front of the class stated loudly, "There is space up here between these two old women."

An audible gasp escaped from the class collectively. The sweet, young instructor immediately knew she had made a terrible mistake. "Oh, I did not mean it to sound that way. I only meant that there was room between these two experienced women. They have been in the class for months. Oh, I am so sorry! That did not sound right!" It did not seem to dawn on anybody that most of the class members had various shades of gray or white hair and were all in the different stages of old. As far as they were all concerned, a mistake had been made, a gaff had occurred, a glaring error had slipped out, and an apology had been made. Whew! All was now well with the world. Let's move on and forget that!

As the class progressed, I began to think. What is wrong with the word old? Why do we shrink from the very mention of it? Why do we use any other word to hopefully soften the concept of age? Why can't aging into *oldness* be a privilege, an honor, a reason to be stunned — even awestruck — that we live in a time where old can become a whole second life, a gift of time? Why can't old mean I have arrived? I am finally comfortable in my own skin. Why can't old mean I have finally figured out a few things and can keep on growing and just being? Believe me, I am not a Polly-anna when it comes to aging. "Getting old is not for pansies," was my father's favorite saying about getting old, or to use my mother's expression, "Oh, right! *The golden years*! Bah humbug!" I have been assisting the elderly for the better part of twenty-four years, so I am under no illusions as to the difficulties aging can encompass. I also took care of my own two parents for years before they died.

Becoming old means losses and changes, some of which can be heartbreaking. Judith Viorst, author of the groundbreaking book, *Necessary Losses*, lists all the losses one encounters as one ages from youth to elder. There may be gradual losses as declining hearing and sight, loss of energies, flexibility (knees, hips), changing appearances (wrinkled skin), and resources. Then there are more major losses as the loss of one's soul mate, a devastating diagnosis, the loss of one's mind, and the loss of close friends to name a few. That being said, it can still be a time of great growth and yes, even joy in having time to appreciate simple beauties, to enjoy friendships, to plan adventures — the list is endless.[2]

All of the three scenarios have one thing in common — denial. The dictionary defines the word, denial, as an assertion that something considered true is false or disbelief in the existence or reality of a thing. It is a re-fusal to recognize or acknowledge. Theories as to why people engage in such behavior are many. In fact, whole books have been written about why people spend time in a state of denial. One theory postulates that people live in denial because of fear — fear of their changing appearance, loss of abilities, and most of all, fear of death, which all of us will face at some point in time. One, of course, hopes that this journey will be trouble free, and for some, it is just that. They are the lucky ones. As Andrew Weil, MD, states in his book, *Healthy Aging*, the ideal is to have a healthy life reaching ones full potential right up to one's death, which would come quickly and swiftly after a long productive life. For many, however, that is not the case and this is where the planning comes into being.[3]

The purpose of this book is to explore just these questions and issues. It is also to lay out a plan for getting old if we are lucky enough! It may come as a surprise to many, but not all of us get to be old. I have been a daily reader of obituaries in the newspaper for decades, partly to keep track of which of my clients have died, but also to see the age of people who died and from what causes. One thing I know for sure — we do *not* all grow old.

When it comes to making plans, there are two kinds of people in the world — those who plan and those who do not plan. In fact, if you say the word "plan" to some people, their eyes glaze over and you know you have lost them. That being said, just think for a moment about taking a trip or a journey, which is what old or aging is all about. It is true some people make infinite detailed plans in preparation for a trip, while others make sketchy plans hoping some serendipitous events will occur without planning. But *everyone* makes some plans even if it is calling the airlines and making airplane reservations. Suppose one made no plans whatsoever before embarking on a trip. The scenario would look something like this as one life partner talks to the other.

"Let's just get in the car and take a trip."

"Where are we going?"

"Oh, let's just get in the car and head out in one direction."

"How long will we be gone?"

"I have no idea."

"What do I pack?"

"Oh, just throw some things into a suitcase — maybe a jacket in case it gets cold."

"Shouldn't we at least have a destination, and what about hotel reservations once we get there?"

"We will just wing it. If there is no room at the inn, we can just sleep in the car."

"Just how much is this going to cost? Can we afford it?"

"I have no idea! We will just have to cross that bridge when we get to it."

I could go on and on with this little scenario, but I think you get the point. Yet this is how the great majority of people begin the *Journey through Old*. Even for non-planners, they still have to make some plans before embarking on a journey. Reservations have to be made if signing up for a tour, and which tour to take depends on cost, dates, and length of trip. One needs to plan what clothing will be necessary for comfort once at the destination. All of this is called planning even for those who consider themselves non-planners.

The *Journey through Old* is no different. It takes planning and discussion with family, who may assist with this journey. It also takes ongoing preparation and re-configuring throughout the journey. If the word, plan, sets your hair on fire, call it something else: a process, a journey, a pathway. The main point is to do something about this journey before you begin traveling.

Take something as simple as our car. Most of us value our cars. We spend time deciding what car to buy, we maintain our cars with regular mechanical checks and oil changes, we protect our cars against theft, we wash and clean our cars, and we have car insurance. Are not our own lives and quality of life on the *Journey through Old* worth at least that much as we plan and spend on our cars? When we value something, we give it our time, our effort, our care, our heart. Value the *Journey through Old!*

PLAN

"Old age is not a disease — it is strength and survivorship, triumph over all kinds of vicissitudes and disappointments, trials and illnesses."
■ MAGGIE KUHN

CHAPTER ONE
THE ADVOCATE

In this Chapter...

- ■ WHAT IS AN ADVOCATE?

- ■ WHY IS AN ADVOCATE NECESSARY?

- ■ SELECTING A GOOD ADVOCATE AND WHAT THEY DO

- ■ PROVIDING BACKUP FOR THE ADVOCATE

- ■ YOUR RESPONSIBILITIES TO YOUR ADVOCATE

- ■ ADVOCATES FOR PETS

WHAT IS AN ADVOCATE?

An advocate is a person who speaks or writes in support of another person. An advocate is a champion, team member, proponent, and backer. Everyone needs an advocate. When we are young, we ideally have a parent as a strong advocate — someone who believes in us when we say we are sick, goes with us to the physician or hospital, and takes care of us in vulnerable events or situations.

As we evolve to adults, friends and spouses often take on this role. As we continue to age, our parents may die, trusted friends may move away, beloved spouses may die, and we may find ourselves without that trusted advocate or support. This situation is compounded by one of the mainstays of our culture — *independence*. In our culture, we are taught from an early age to be independent and self-sufficient. We go away to college, we move across our big country, or even settle in other countries. We are restless people. Some adults remain childfree or are estranged from their adult children. Because we were raised to be independent, we find it very difficult if not impossible to seek advocacy of any kind when we need it most.

WHY IS AN ADVOCATE NECESSARY?

The resulting isolation and reluctance for help and advocacy is a vicious cycle: the more alone we are, the more elder adults fear losing their independence. They refuse any outside help or advocacy. In spite of efforts from family, adult children, friends, and concerned neighbors, elders may shun all efforts to reach out and help them. When we add denial and fear of aging, elders set themselves up for something bad to happen. This is the reason for advocacy. Advocacy attempts to prevent some of these bad things from occurring by finding problems early, by being another set of eyes and ears when accompanying an elder to a health care provider, by being a watchful participant/companion on the journey, and alerting family members or a physician early when a decline or change in condition is noted.

Often, concerned family members may turn to the primary care physician. Physicians are hard-pressed to provide the type of oversight needed in these situations. They can generally provide a Band-Aid to help the situation by saying, "Okay, I will talk to your parents." For those elders with short-term memory loss, "the talk" only lasts a few minutes and then is forgotten. The physician is a critical member of the care team, but does not have time to provide the daily oversight and planning many elders need.

This situation may prompt an adult child, physician, pastor, attorney, or neighbor to call a care manager. This is usually a registered nurse or social worker working independently or with a home care agency or elder law attorney. The care manager's job is to set an appointment with the family in the elder's home, do an assessment, establish trust, and develop an individualized plan of care. This plan of care addresses the topics of household assistance in the form of meal preparation, light housekeeping, personal care, medication management, needed doctor/dental appointments, elder law attorney referrals, and documentation assistance (wills, trust, durable power of attorney for health care, financial durable power, financial planning).

The care manager provides plans and structures that enable elders to remain safely in their home, which may or may not include paid caregiver help. If caregivers are needed, the care manager will create a plan of care for the caregiver, and monitor these caregivers to assure they are following their plan of care. The care manager may bring disparate family members together and eventually formulate a plan that may involve various family members assisting the elder often augmented by agency or private caregivers. The care manager is a communication lifeline to family members concerned for the elder's welfare. Ongoing oversight and monitoring of the elder is a cornerstone of the care manager profession.

We say it takes a village to raise a child, but it also takes a village to shepherd the elderly in our society so they are able to live happily and safely in their own environment.

Advocacy takes many forms, both paid and unpaid. An elder law attorney once asked me, "Susan, where are the nice middle-aged women who used to care for the elderly without pay?"

I could not believe what he was asking, but I knew he was serious. "Well," I answered, "those nice middle-aged women are now our teachers, attorneys, physicians, nurses, business women, and police. They do not work for nothing. This includes caregivers for the elderly."

This is not to say there are no unpaid caregivers. There are many, and they are unsung heroes. Unpaid caregivers and advocates are usually adult children who live nearby, a caring neighbor, or someone from the elder's faith community. A son or daughter, for example, may drop in on their parent as needed, assist with medication, accompany the parent to physician appointments, pay bills, and help with meals, housekeeping and personal care. The list is long, and although adult children may start out with good intentions, it may eventually become too much. Most adult children have no knowledge of aging or dementia and may, themselves, be in deep denial regarding their parent's condition.

SELECTING A GOOD ADVOCATE AND WHAT THEY DO

So how does one go about finding an advocate? The following criteria can help you in making this decision:

■ The person, when asked, should agree they are willing to accept this responsibility.

Do not assume that everyone wants to do this. In finding an advocate, it may be an adult child living nearby, a neighbor/friend, or a member of your faith community. Ask people who may also have an advocate. Ask your physician if they know of someone, ask your faith community leader if they know someone.

Some faith communities have people who volunteer for these tasks. You can call your Area Agency on Aging (AAA), a federal program at 1-800-677-1116, or online at www.eldercare.gov, to locate your local resources. They may have a list of volunteers or paid people to suggest. If all else fails, you may have to hire someone through your local home care agency.

■ The advocate should live nearby.

An adult child or relative who lives far away should only be the back-up advocate. You want someone nearby who can accompany you to the hospital or be present at the physician's office to take notes and help you sort out information.

■ The advocate should be someone you know and trust and agrees with your wishes and directives. (We will talk about this in greater detail in the next chapters.)

■ The advocate should have a car to transport you if necessary.

■ The advocate should be willing to keep a copy of your medical information in the form of a Personal Health Record (PHR). (For more information, see "Documentation" on page 21.) Your up-to-date PHR should accompany you whenever you go to your doctor, other health provider (i.e., dentist, podiatrist), emergency room, or hospital.

■ The advocate should have contact information of people to notify in case of an emergency, decline, *or* if the advocate feels they can no longer provide this service.

■ Using daily phone calls, emails, and/or regular brief visits, an advocate should monitor your safety and whether you can manage your needs.

Don't just assume a friend or neighbor will be your advocate if something happens. This assumption was made about my own parents. They lived in a retirement community and had wonderful neighbors. Their neighbors, Jane and Fred, were their closest friends. Fred died suddenly without warning after a fifty-year marriage, and Jane was alone for the first time in her life. As time went on, Jane became very frail, being overwhelmed by the details of living alone. At first, both of my parents pitched in trying to shore up Jane. My father taught her to write a check and pay bills, things she had never done and had never planned to do. My mother helped with the groceries and cooking as Jane was not eating. My father's role gradually faded away, but my mother's role increased. Jane lost weight and was falling on a regular basis. My mother was so busy taking care of Jane, her own health began to fail. My father eventually called the daughter who lived across the country. He explained they were no longer able to play this role of caregiver/advocate (having never been asked), and Jane needed more help than they could give. The daughter came immediately and took her mother to live near her. This situation happens frequently.

When my father died after almost sixty years of marriage, I stayed with my mother following his funeral to clean up financial details and provide some support and companionship. After I exhausted my paid vacation from my full-time work, I returned home in a neighboring state. I called my mother every day for a while and then tapered off to several times a week. Over the phone, she sounded like she was managing, and we talked many times about grief and how to get through that process. About three months after my father died, I got a call from her in the middle of the night, stating she had fallen and could not get up. I immediately called the neighbor and requested they call 911. I dressed and headed for the airport.

When I arrived at my mother's home, I was shocked at her appearance. She had lost about thirty pounds and looked emaciated. She was confused following the fall, and clearly was not herself mentally. She cried often and could not seem to eat or hydrate herself. She had fallen over a chair in the night trying to get to the bathroom and had broken all her ribs on one side. It was then that the neighbors came to me one by one and requested that I not leave my mother, as they just could not continue to care for her. Unbeknownst to me, they had been caring for her since the day I had left!

PROVIDING BACKUP FOR THE ADVOCATE

These two examples demonstrate that advocates can be a great help, but there comes a time when more help is needed than an advocate can give. Your advocate always needs a backup family member to talk to, and plans should be in place when simple advocacy no longer fills the need. When care needs overwhelm simple advocacy (usually unpaid services from a neighbor, friend, or nearby family member for a few hours a week or less), then paid advocacy from an agency or care manager may be necessary.

There is no hard and fast rule as to when paid advocacy is needed as it is often up to the advocate as how much time and energy they can devote. There are guidelines, however, based on Activities of Daily Living (ADL) deficits and Instrumental Activities of Daily Living (IADL) deficits. (For more information, see "Safety" on page 35.) Searching online for *elder advocacy* and *care management* services will bring up agencies or individuals in your geographic area offering this service. The National Association of Professional Geriatric Care

Managers can be accessed at www.caremanager.org for a list of local care managers. Individual care managers generally charge approximately $100.00 per hour. This cost may be less if it comes as part of a caregiver service from an agency. Your physician or faith community may also provide recommendations.

YOUR RESPONSIBILITIES TO YOUR ADVOCATE

■ Keep your advocate's PHR copy updated with any changes.

■ Inform your advocate of issues or problems as they arise. Do not let issues fester and get worse.

■ Arrange a time each day to touch base via phone, email, or brief visit.

ADVOCATES FOR PETS

As we talk about advocates for elders, do not forget to include plans and an advocate for beloved pets. This is a much-neglected area of elder care and causes last minute panic during a crisis. Make plans now for your pet while you are able and not in the midst of a crisis. Find an advocate ahead of time who will take care of your pet if you are suddenly taken ill or hospitalized. Provide funds and supplies for that person to use plus the name and contact number of the veterinarian. One client I had for several years had made wonderful plans and secured several advocates for her beloved dog, but had made none for herself. The dog, Weedie, had a dog walker who took her out twice a day, another person took Weedie to her standing appointment with a groomer every month, and a third advocate took Weedie to her vet appointment every six months. There was also another family who would take Weedie if the elder died. Weedie was a very lucky dog!

TASK LIST

☐ FIND YOUR ADVOCATE AND BACK-UP ADVOCATE.

☐ GIVE YOUR ADVOCATE COPIES OF YOUR PERSONAL HEALTH RECORD AND YOUR ADVANCED DIRECTIVE.

☐ ESTABLISH A MONITORING PLAN FOR YOU AND YOUR ADVOCATE.

*"The word 'now' is like a bomb
through the window, and it ticks."*
■ ARTHUR MILLER

CHAPTER TWO
DOCUMENTATION

In this Chapter...

■ THE DREADED PAPERWORK AND WHO PREPARES IT

■ PERSONAL HEALTH RECORD

■ WILLS AND TRUSTS

■ DURABLE POWER OF ATTORNEY FOR HEALTH CARE
(ADVANCED DIRECTIVES)

■ DURABLE POWER OF ATTORNEY FOR FINANCES

■ ORGANIZING YOUR DOCUMENTS

THE DREADED PAPERWORK
AND WHO PREPARES IT

Documentation is another word for the dreaded word *paperwork*. For many, just the mention of "documentation" makes their brain turn to mush. People would rather stick a hot poker in their eye. However, as the Nike ad says, "*Just Do It!*" You have heard the expression, "The job's not done till the paperwork is completed." Nothing is truer in the planning for old. It is a task that should not be put off.

One of the easiest ways is to contact an elder law attorney and/or an estate-planning attorney and simply have him or her take care of all the documents at once with the exception of the PHR, which you will have to complete yourself. Obviously there is a cost involved in this process, but it is the easiest, and one I highly recommend. Short of that, however, elders can do this by themselves if they have the time and inclination.

Fees for attorney services, at a minimum, will cost several hundred dollars, and will depend on the complexity of the estate, location of your residence, and how many hours are required to complete the task. Doing it yourself is *not* a job for elders if they have short-term memory loss or any kind of dementia. The time to do this is *now* and not when you are in the middle of a crisis, which is guaranteed to happen on the *Journey through Old*. A helpful online resource is www.naela.org, which stands for the National Academy of Elder Law Attorneys and provides a search for an attorney in your area. Ask others that you know if they use or know of an elder law attorney or estate-planning attorney.

The documents that are needed are as follows:

■ Personal Health Record (PHR)

■ wills and trusts

■ Durable Power of Attorney for Health Care (DPAHC or advanced directives)

■ Durable Power of Attorney for Finances (POA finance)

Once these documents are established, it is important to distribute copies to the appropriate people who the elder has designated plus let advocates and family know where the originals are kept. Many of you have heard of someone dying, but no one can find the will or trust much less any other important documents. This is one of the devastating results of denial and the cause of much grief and frustration on the part of those who are left to deal with this chaos after a death.

PERSONAL HEALTH RECORD (PHR)

The purpose of a PHR is to keep everyone who may be treating you on the same sheet of music. (This is a document that an elder law attorney *cannot* help you establish.) Only you know your health history, medication, and diagnosis. A PHR is a record of the following:

■ Allergies to foods, drugs, or environment.

■ All your vital statistics — name, address, phone numbers, email address (many physicians now communicate using email), birth date, social security number, Medicare/Medicaid number, supplementary or other insurance information, height, weight, blood type, current immunizations, alcohol/smoking use, and medical devices such as a pacemaker.

■ Your past medical history, surgeries, injuries, diagnoses, and hospitalizations.

■ Your last MD office visit.

■ Current physicians and dentists: their names, addresses, phone numbers, and specialty.

■ Your pharmacy: the phone number, and whether or not they deliver.

■ A complete list of all your current medications including dosages, times, date prescribed, reason prescribed, who prescribed, plus over-the-counters (like aspirin, Tylenol), vitamins, supplements, herbals.

■ Names, addresses, and phone numbers of your advocates, family members, and other emergency contacts.

■ Copies of your durable power of attorney for health care, organ donor authorization, and your durable power of attorney for finance.

You can use forms for a PHR on the Internet, devise your own form, or handprint the information in a notebook. **The important thing is to keep it updated!** When a medication is added, deleted, or the dosage is changed, *update* your record. When you receive a new diagnosis and treatment, *update* your record. A record is worthless if the information is no longer valid.

There are excellent resources online for PHRs. One of the best I have found is myphr.com. It is a site run by the American Health Information Management Association AHIMA (AHIMA). Here you can print out a comprehensive PHR form or you can find resources on this web site to create an online version of a PHR.

Take this record with you whenever you go to your physician, dentist, eye doctor, emergency room, or hospital. A copy of this record should be with your advocate with instructions to always bring this document when accompanying you to any appointment or to the hospital. A trusted family member should also have a copy of this record. When you make changes to the record, do not forget to copy them as well. It takes effort to keep it updated, but it is well worth the trouble.

Not only can it save precious minutes in an emergency room, but also can prevent costly mistakes. In any health emergency or event, you may be treated or seen by several medical specialists. When specialists have the same consistent information in the PHR, costly and sometimes calamitous outcomes can be prevented. Here is one example of why this is so valuable.

Alice was an elderly patient that I had care managed for a period of months. She had a chronic and complex psychiatric history and almost no short-term memory. She was being cared for in an adult family home. No family was nearby. Early one morning, I got a call from the home manager that Alice was not doing well, and she thought I should see her. At the adult family home, I assessed her and called 911. I followed in my car and accompanied Alice into the emergency room. I presented her PHR to the emergency room physician who reviewed it while the nurse prepared Alice for an examination. The physician said, "You have no idea how helpful this is! We would have been stabbing in the dark with this patient because she has no memory. So many patients come to the hospital, and we have no history of their past diagnoses, their medications, or who to contact." The Emergency Room physician was able to resolve Alice's problem quickly and efficiently, and Alice was soon on her way home. A PHR saves valuable time plus assures more positive outcomes for the elder.

WILLS AND TRUSTS

A will is a document that states your wishes for what happens to your assets after your death. A trust may have provisions for both before you die and after.

The regulations and laws vary from state to state, and this is truly a job for an attorney who lives in your area. Always change your will/trust when your circumstances change, like a move to another state or a change in marital status. It is a good idea to review your will/trust with your attorney on a regular basis.

Let me give you an example of what can happen without a will/trust. A close friend suddenly lost her mother. Her mother had been traveling with her new husband, and on returning home, told her spouse she did not feel well. She went into her bedroom to lie down and unexpectedly died of a heart attack. She did not have a will! Her new husband inherited her estate — all of it. Six weeks later, he suddenly died of a heart attack, and his estate (including his wife's assets) went to his only son, thus excluding his wife's two daughters. This is just one example of what can happen when we do not put a plan in place for growing old and for our demise.

Everyone needs a will/trust regardless of one's age. There are materials in most bookstores and on the Internet to draw up your own will, but I still strongly advise you to seek the professional assistance of an elder law attorney or estate attorney. The main thing is *just do it!* and do it without delay.

When arranging for a will and/or a trust, appoint someone to be the executor of the will. This is a person you trust who will make sure the provisions of the will/trust are carried out as directed in the documents. Make sure that the person you appoint accepts this responsibility and knows what is involved.

It does no good to have a will/trust when no one knows the location of the document. The will/trust copy should be kept with your attorney. You should have a copy, and your family or executor should know where the copy is located plus how to contact the attorney. The original should be in a safety deposit box and arrangements made to allow family members access to the box on your death.

DURABLE POWER OF ATTORNEY FOR HEALTH CARE (DPOAHC)

This is also known as *advanced directives*. In these documents you state what *your* wishes are should you be unable to speak for yourself. The circumstances where this might apply are myriad, including any loss of consciousness. All hospitals will ask you for a copy of your advanced directive on admission or will urge you to fill one out if you do not have one. ***This document applies to the hospital setting and your physician***. In fact, your physician should have a copy of your advanced directive in his or her office with your records.

This document can vary from state to state, and physicians usually have the blank documents in their offices if you request one. Forms can also be located on the Internet. The ideal process is to discuss your wishes with your physician, your family, and/or advocate. The form will ask you to designate a primary spokesperson and an alternate spokesperson to speak for you if you are unable to speak for yourself.

You will also need to decide what you want done if there is no hope of recovery. Do you want to be kept alive *with all the stops pulled out,* or do you want comfort measures including pain relief only, to allow the dying process to proceed naturally? The task of your appointed spokesperson is to make sure that *your* wishes are honored. Your signature and witness signatures are required. Your physician does *not* have to sign this particular document but does need a copy on file. You can change the form at any time, but just make sure your doctor and your advocates know of your changes. Redistribute the new form.

Pulling out the stops and thus prolonging life includes the following:

Cardiopulmonary resuscitation. CPR is an attempt to restart the heart and lungs, which have stopped working. It involves chest compressions, medications, electric shock, and possibly a tube placed in the windpipe for breathing.

Ventilator. This is a machine that breathes for a patient who is unable to breathe on his or her own.

Artificial nutrition and hydration. This is the administration of food or fluids either through a tube into the stomach or through an intravenous line (IV).

Here is what can happen when there is no plan or advanced directive in place. One night, I received a call from one of the night nurses on my staff. She had been called out to a home where a 98-year-old patient was no longer responsive and seemed to be dying. The family was in crisis and in full panic mode. Half the family felt the patient should just be allowed to die at home peacefully. The other half of the family felt strongly that 911 should be called and the patient taken to the hospital for life saving measures. No plans were in place.

The nurse arrived at the home to find a family tragically divided and raging at each other about what to do. The nurse called me to seek direction as to how she should proceed. In that particular county, the rule was that if medical personnel were called, and there was no DO NOT RECUSITATE order in the house and no advanced directive, 911 must be called, the patient transported to the hospital, and measures taken to keep the patient alive. This was a tragedy as half the family stated that the patient had disclosed verbally she did not want to go to the hospital and definitely did not want life saving measures.

To clear up a common misconception: A *Do Not Resuscitate* (DNR) order is *in addition* to an advanced directive. An advanced directive is for the hospital setting. The DNR is for the home setting. If a patient is in a state of decline due to a chronic or terminal illness and may anticipate dying at home, a DNR order *signed by the phy-*

sician must be in the home setting if the patient wants only comfort measures and does not want life saving measures. If 911 is called and you show them the DNR order, they can transport the patient to the hospital without performing lifesaving measures. Many patients in this condition are on hospice, which takes care of all these paperwork duties ahead of time. However, if not on hospice, the patient and the advocates need to be sure these documents are in order and kept in a place where everyone can find them. Most paramedics are trained to look in the refrigerator for the DNR order, which is kept in a container (VIAL OF LIFE) in the refrigerator. You can buy these vials of life in most drug stores.

In the case of my own mother who was declining in her nineties, I had the vial of life in place plus a note on the refrigerator that the DNR was inside. My mother was actually eating dinner in her facility dining room when she literally died walking out of the dining room. 911 paramedics were immediately called and came barreling into the facility to start CPR. Fortunately, my mother's close friend hovered over the paramedics and said, "You had better not do that! Her daughter has posted a sign on her refrigerator not to do that!" A fireman quickly went to her room, found the DNR, and all life saving measures were stopped. I am profoundly grateful to my mother's friend. My mother was adamant that she did not want life saving measures at this point in her life and had made that clear to all of us.

In some states, there is a form called a POLST. This stands for Physician Orders for Life Sustaining Treatment. This form combines both the advanced directive and the DNR. A physician must sign this form.

To summarize, if you are in reasonable health and do not have a serious illness, you only need the advanced directive (DPOAHC) for the hospital if you unexpectedly find yourself in that setting. If you are in declining health at home and do NOT want extraordinary measures to keep you alive at the end of life, you need a DNR.

DURABLE POWER OF ATTORNEY FOR FINANCES

This form allows your designated person to make financial decisions and pay bills on your behalf should you become unable to perform those tasks. The tasks can include managing personal property, banking, bill paying, stocks, personal and family maintenance, retirement plans, and tax matters. Your designated person should be a trusted advocate or family member who is willing to accept these tasks when requested. In some cases this document requires a notarized signature. An elder law attorney can create this document for you; however, you may do it by yourself.

There are online resources that assist you to create these documents if that is the path you choose. Some are free and some require a fee. These resources are as follows:

- www.nolo.com

- www.lawdepot.com

- www.rocketlawyer.com

- There are also several legal kits on Amazon.com that have both paper forms you can order as well as applications that one can use to create forms on your computer.

ORGANIZING YOUR DOCUMENTS

After you have all of these documents completed, it is important to have them plus other important papers and information in a place where your advocates, family members, or executors can find them. You can do this in one of two ways. Computers are a wonderful tool to keep all of this information in one place and make updates as needed. Just make sure your designated people know where and how to access this information. A simple notebook is also another way. Just make sure everyone involved knows where the notebook is located. *Keep all information updated.* The information you will want to keep in one place and tell your family, advocates, and/or executors is as follows:

■ Location of all the important documents.

■ Names and contact information of people you want notified if you become ill or die.

■ Names and contact information of all physicians and dentist.

■ Name and contact information of faith leader.

■ Location of house and car keys.

■ Name and number of pharmacy.

■ Name and number of elder law attorney, estate attorney, and/or financial advisor.

■ List of all financial accounts with name and number of contact person: checking, saving, assets.

■ List of credit cards.

■ List of all insurances including long term care insurance and where the policies are kept.

■ Written instructions and advocate contact information for your pet.

In summary, documentation helps you stay in control of your life. It also brings great peace of mind to have made these decisions in a state of calm when you can think clearly rather than in a state of crisis and chaos.

TASK LIST

☐ FIND AN ELDER LAW ATTORNEY TO CREATE YOUR DOCUMENTS.

☐ DISCUSS AND ESTABLISH YOUR ADVANCED DIRECTIVE WITH YOUR PHYSICIAN AND FAMILY.

☐ ESTABLISH A SAFE PLACE FOR YOUR DOCUMENTS AND PROVIDE YOUR DESIGNATED ADVOCATES/FAMILY ACCESS TO THESE DOCUMENTS.

☐ IF LIFE CIRCUMSTANCES CHANGE, UPDATE DOCUMENTS.

☐ CREATE YOUR PHR.

*"The need for change bulldozed a
road down the center of my mind."*
■ MAYA ANGELOU

CHAPTER THREE
SAFETY

In this Chapter...

PLANNING FOR SAFETY

Safety is one of the most crucial issues to address as one ages. Aging is a subjective process — some people start aging in their fifties or earlier and others may not show much sign of aging until they are in their seventies or older. Science tells us the aging process begins about the age of twenty-six which is the age when our bodies stop building up (anabolic) and start tearing down, (catabolic.) A science professor once said, "You may think you are still young in your twenties, but in truth, after you reach twenty-six, it is downhill all the way!" Much laughter ensued, but his point was never forgotten.

So when *do* you think about the journey to old. Financially, you begin to think about it when you get your first job that offers some sort of retirement plan. Many companies may also offer you long term care insurance as a benefit. If you are going to have enough money to carry you through retirement, it takes planning and saving starting in your twenties. A will should also be considered if you have a job and assets plus are starting a family. Aside from those two items (money for retirement and a will), you should start looking at the journey to old certainly by your mid to late fifties. This is a very subjective number, but for the majority of people, this is probably realistic.

Safety issues come in many guises. The following divides safety into manageable pieces:

◀ Fall prevention

◀ Physical safety in the home

◀ Physical safety outside the home

- Elder driving safety

- Medication safety

- Alcohol/drug safety

- Safety from scams

Elder driving safety, medication safety, alcohol/drug safety, and scam prevention have their own chapters.

Most people do not think about their safety in terms of their aging until *after* something bad happens. The scenario looks something like this. John is seventy-two years old, and he and his wife have noticed that he seems to be tripping lately. He may trip on a throw rug or the leg of a table. He has prostate issues and uses the bathroom frequently, especially at night. One night in his effort to get to the bathroom quickly, he trips on the throw rug in the bathroom and falls hitting his head on the sink. He now has a concussion, a scalp laceration, and a broken hip.

After John comes home from the hospital, the doctor orders a Medicare physical therapist to come to the home and do a safety evaluation. The physical therapist advises the family to place grab bars in the bathroom by the toilet and the shower, remove all throw rugs, and increase lighting, plus other safety equipment and recommendations. This is a prime example of closing the barn door after the horse is out. Falls are common in the elderly and preventable! It takes a plan, diligence, and effort to prevent falls.

It is very frustrating for a registered nurse or a physical therapist to go to people's homes either before or after a patient has fallen, make the recommendations, and get fierce resistance from the patient and the family. For some unknown reason, people seem inordinately attached to one of their biggest hazards, their throw rugs! "Why, I have had that throw rug in that place since 1952. That throw rug came across the prairie in a covered wagon. I see no reason to remove it now." Or here is another one. "I am *not* going to put up grab bars in my bathroom. It will ruin the décor and besides, my guests will think that I am old." A woman who had just returned from the hospital after a fall in her bathroom, which fractured her hip and broke one arm, made this last comment. Somehow thinking about and taking action before an accident seems an anathema to most people, and for some, they do not want to take action even after a fall. This is a sad illustration of being in denial about aging. Accidents are almost always preventable if we take the necessary actions to prevent them.

FALLS: THEIR CAUSES AND PREVENTION

Falls can be catastrophic for an elder and often the damage cannot be undone. Here is a pop quiz.

Question: What's the common thread among these people?

◀ Actor William Holden

◀ Comedian George Burns

◀ Publisher Katherine Graham

◀ Journalist David Brinkley

◀ Literary legend Kurt Vonnegut.

Answer: They all died from complications of a fall.[1] In other words, the actual fall may not have caused the death, but complications as pneumonia or other infections are the actual cause of death, which resulted from the fall.

FACTS ABOUT FALLS

Here are some sobering facts about falls.

- More than one of every three adults aged sixty-five and older falls each year.

- One in ten will suffer a serious injury such as a fractured hip.

- More than forty percent of those hospitalized from hip fracture cannot live independently and do not return home.

- Falls are also the leading cause of injury, hospital visits due to trauma, and death from an injury among this age group. According to the CDC (Centers for Disease Control), in 2010, 2.3 million nonfatal fall injuries among the elderly were treated in emergency rooms and more than 662,000 were hospitalized, resulting in a cost of $30 billion.

- In 2003, the total direct cost for falls for this group was approximately $27.3 billion. By 2020, it is expected to reach $43.8 billion.

- Fifty-five percent of falls occur in the home and most can be prevented.

- Increased falls are in direct proportion to aging.

- Recurrence factor. Once an elder falls, they are three times more likely to fall again.

■ If falls recur, the elder becomes more fearful, exercise decreases due to fear, and weakness ensues, leading to more falls.

■ Most home accidents occur on level flooring.[2]

REASONS THE ELDERLY FALL

Here are the main reasons why elders fall.

Decline or loss of balance. Decline in balance has a myriad of causes such as decline in vision and hearing, medication side effects, certain diseases, peripheral neuropathy (loss of feeling in lower extremities), degenerative joint disease in knees and hips, nutritional deficiencies, electrolyte imbalance, middle or inner ear problems, dizziness from varied causes, stroke, alcohol and drug abuse, or urinary tract infections. *Always have any deficiency evaluated by a physician!* Do not assume that it is because the elder is just getting old. Sometimes something as simple as changing a medication solves the problem.

Urinary or bowel urgency. Many accidents occur in the home because of rushing to get to the bathroom before an accident occurs. This often happens at night when we do not turn on the light or put on slippers. We rush to the bathroom at night in the dark in our bare feet and trip. A physician should evaluate any bowel or bladder problem. If no discernable cause can be found, using a bedside commode would save many a hip. This equipment enables the elder to slide from bed to commode and back to bed without hurrying to a bathroom down the hall or across the room. If the commode is not needed during the day, it is easily folded up and put in a closet until bedtime.

Physical barriers. Clear pathways of obstacles. Some homes use the hallway as storage space. You can hardly walk down the hallway without encountering a box or a pile of clothes. This is especially true if grandchildren are living in the home. Keep electrical cords secured along walls and not crossing over a pathway. People kick off their shoes when they come into the house, or when they sit down. They trip over the shoes when they get up. If you are going to put books, shoes, and dishes on the floor beside your chair or couch, move them to one side so as not to fall over them when you get up.

Stairs. All stairs, inside and out, are hazards and should have handrails on both sides even for a few steps. Stair treads also prevent slipping. Stairs should be well lit. One hand should be free to hold onto the railing. Do *not* fill both hands and arms with laundry or other items and then proceed up or down stairs. Only carry what you can hold in one hand or arm and hold onto the railing with the other.

Inadequate lighting. An elder needs two to three times stronger lighting to see than a younger person needs. It is amazing to see people use 40- or 60-watt light bulbs to save money, which is grossly inadequate for an elder with or without vision deficiencies. Use a minimum of 100 to 150 watts or higher. At night, the use of night-lights is also essential, especially in the bathroom and in the hallway, which the elder may use to get to the bathroom.

Slipping on throw rugs and wet floors. Get rid of throw or scatter rugs. Clean up any spills immediately. In the bathroom, get a bath mat with a rubber backing that will not slip out from under a person.

Inadequate footwear. Shoes should be worn at all times and should support the foot. If wearing slippers, obtain slippers with a sole and some support. Adequate footwear can prevent falls and improve balance. Low or flat-heeled shoes that give firm support are best. Your podiatrist can give you advice on what kind of shoes to wear and where to find them in your area. Putting on slippers at night also can improve balance and prevent falls.

Difficult to reach items. Stretching on tiptoe or even worse, using a chair or stool to reach high objects is a hazard. Place hard to reach items within easy reach. Help may be needed to relocate high or difficult to reach items into areas that are easy to reach. *Avoid* stepladders, stools, and standing on chairs.

Weakness and debility due to lack of exercise. *Keep moving* is a mantra we all should have from our earliest age. Exercise keeps us fit, provides energy, helps our lungs and heart, improves our balance, and thus prevents falls. Lack of exercise weakens joints, muscles, bones, and contributes to falls. Senior centers offer exercise classes specifically geared toward the elder client, as do gyms. Privately hired physical therapists and personal trainers for the elderly can also be of great help in keeping an elder in shape.

WAYS TO PREVENT FALLS

Falls can be prevented by the following approach:

Obtain a fall history. This is usually done by the physician and includes a physical assessment, medication assessment, vision assessment, gait observation, and fall history. The physician then makes a referral to physical therapy and occupational therapy.

Consult professionals. Four professionals are needed to determine why falls are occurring: the physician, physical therapist, occupational therapist, and care manager. Any reasons for loss or decline of balance need to be corrected if possible.

Work with a therapist. A physical therapist and occupational therapist will establish a home exercise program, assess the home for safety issues, and make recommendations. A care manager sees that the recommendations are accomplished, monitors the program, and teaches the caregiver, if present.

Work with a personal trainer. A personal trainer may be needed to insure compliance with the home exercise program on an ongoing basis.

Modify the home. Environmental modifications (reduce home hazards) and procuring adaptive equipment (DME) need to be completed.

Education. The elder will need instruction, training, and behavior changes to prevent future falls.

Pets. How pets are kept in the home should be evaluated to determine if they could be a cause of falls. It is not unusual for an elder to trip over their beloved pet.

OTHER MATTERS OF PHYSICAL SAFETY

Planning for safety should address issues that can affect the elder, both inside and outside the home.

NATURAL EMERGENCIES

Everyone, regardless of age, should have an emergency plan to get out of a house that is on fire, flooded, in an earthquake, tornado, or severe weather. Several of my older patients died in fires, and earthquakes in California have stranded others. Everyone should have an emergency plan on how to get an elder and pet out of the house quickly if necessary. I have seen many elders who are housebound, wheelchair bound, or bed bound with no way for them to manage an exit either due to stairs they cannot maneuver or decks with no stairs.

There should always be an emergency supply kit in every home with emergency numbers, functioning flash light, cell phone, water and food for three days, extra pet food, oxygen back up if on oxygen, and enough medications for several days. Sit down with your family members and work out an emergency plan as to how the elder will safely get out of the house in an emergency. The house needs to have multiple exits, and railings and ramps leading from exits to the ground level. Fire departments have labels to affix onto a window to indicate a frail elder and/or pet live there.

MEMORY DEFICIT

Memory deficits affect all aspects of an elder's life. Have any deficits evaluated by a physician and possibly a neurologist. In terms of safety, the kitchen is one of the most dangerous places for the memory-impaired adult. Forgetting to turn off the stove or oven is common and has led to some devastating outcomes.

When an advocate or family member is visiting an elder, look at the kitchen. Do you see signs of pots, pans, or teapots with burn marks or even the bottoms burned out of the container? Do you notice burn marks on the wall behind the stovetop? This is a difficult issue for elders living alone, and sometimes it may be necessary to disarm the stove or oven and just make the microwave available to the elder. Electric teapots that turn off automatically are also a preventive measure.

INCLEMENT WEATHER

Rain-slick walkways and snow and ice are the cause of many falls for everyone, not just the elderly. For all of us, Yaktrax are inexpensive devices to wear over our shoes in snow and ice; they make walking easier without fear of falling. Keep outside steps and walkways free of ice and snow.

SMOKE DETECTORS

Installing smoke detectors is crucial in any home. According to the United States Fire Administration of the Department of Homeland Security, the United States death rate from fires is the largest in the industrialized world, killing nearly 3,000 people a year and injuring about 20,000 people. Most of these deaths and injuries occur in homes without an operating smoke alarm, and are therefore preventable.

Added to these alarming statistics is the loss of approximately 100 firefighters who are killed fighting these fires plus the resulting property losses of almost $11 billion a year. In the course of my career, three of my elders have died in house fires. Two died by taking sleeping medications and then smoking in bed. The other died from a malfunctioning furnace fire.

Smoke alarms are only as good as the vigilance paid to keep them in working order. Care managers recommend that the smoke alarm batteries be changed on the elder's birthday as a way of remembering this important task.

Smoke alarms should be installed in the following places:

■ Inside each bedroom and on every level of the home including the basement.

■ In the living room, den, and family room.

■ Install more than ten feet from the kitchen to minimize false alarms from kitchen heat.

■ Do NOT install near windows, doors, or ducts where drafts could cause a malfunction.

For additional information about smoke alarms, go to: www.nfpa.org/safety-information/for-consumers/fire-and-safety-equipment/smoke-alarms/installing-and-maintaining-smoke-alarms

GETTING ASSISTANCE WITH THESE SAFETY MEASURES

A care manager or other professional like a physical therapist can be hired to perform a home safety assessment and make recommendations to correct deficiencies. These may be as simple as smoke detectors, brighter light bulbs, or a night-light. Months later the deficiency is still present and no effort has been made to remedy the issue. It almost takes something bad to happen in order to initiate action.

Choose a date and time and commit to carefully assessing the living environment. Make a list of the corrections, and get the necessary equipment to get it done. If you do not have the time or know-how, call a handy person or a contractor that does work for elders in their homes. Senior centers usually have a list of such people as does the Alzheimer's Association.

SAFETY EQUIPMENT

Sometimes an individual may need safety equipment and preventive measures not because the aging process requires it on a permanent basis but because of an impending surgery. I will use my own experience as an example.

STORY: AN OUNCE OF PREVENTION...

 As a weekend hiker/walker, it became more difficult to hike up and down hills due to increasing knee pain. I tried to put off any medical intervention until I could not stand it. Walking became difficult and painful. In my mid-sixties, I was active and did not want to give up the outside activities I so enjoyed.

I decided it was finally time for a knee replacement. My orthopedic surgeon stated I was past due for such a procedure and gave me a notebook of information to help me prepare for the pre- and post-operative procedure. For eight weeks before the surgery I was to do leg exercises to strengthen the muscles around my knee. Post operatively, I was to have grab bars installed in my bathroom, a shower chair, a hand-held shower, a bedside commode, toilet raiser, cane, and a walker.

I hired a handy person I had heard about through word of mouth, and who specialized in helping the elderly install safety equipment. He installed the grab bars, assembled all the other equipment, and got everything in place. By the time he left, the hand-held shower and shower chair were in place, the toilet raisers were installed in two bathrooms, the bedside commode was assembled and placed beside my bed.

When the surgeon discharged me from the hospital, he said, "Hopefully all your home equipment is in place. Do Not Fall!" All equipment and safety measures were in place, and my post-op course was uneventful with a great outcome. Within three months, I had my second knee replaced and was hiking in Europe five months later. Most of the equipment now hangs in my garage, but I still have my grab bars, which I use to get in and out of my shower safely.

DURABLE MEDICAL EQUIPMENT (DME)

There are many assistive devices to remedy deficiencies and barriers. These devices are called assistive devices or Durable Medical Equipment (DME), and can be obtained from drug stores or DME companies. They are usually ordered by a physical therapist, occupational therapist, and physician after an elder comes back home from an accident. However, anyone can get this equipment or request the piece of equipment from their doctor.

Medicare will pay for some of this equipment with a doctor's order, but the equipment is very basic. For example, when it came time for my mother to have a walker, I wanted a walker with wheels, brakes, and a seat for her to sit on when she got fatigued. I knew she was ready for a walker as she was beginning to hold onto furniture and walls for support as she walked.

The walker I chose was twice as expensive as the basic walker Medicare paid for — you know the kind, basic gunmetal grey with tennis balls inserted on the walker legs instead of wheels. The DME company secured the doctor's order, billed Medicare for the basic walker, and I paid the extra for the "Cadillac" variety.

Your DME company will be able to tell you what Medicare will and will not pay for. Some common pieces of equipment are toilet raisers, bedside commodes, grab bars, reachers, sock aids, large handled utensils, shower benches and chairs, hand-held showers, side rails for beds, lift chairs, and wheelchairs. The list is endless. Whatever issue an elder is having, there is a piece of equipment to assist. These DME companies usually have knowledgeable people who are ready to assist you in choosing the right piece of equipment, and the need for such equipment is based on the assessment of Activities of Daily Living (ADLs) and Instrumental Activities of Daily Living (IADLs).

ACTIVITIES OF DAILY LIVING AND INSTRUMENTAL ADLs

Often the question is asked, "How do I know if my loved one needs help or needs equipment?" This is an excellent question, and needs to be continually asked as aging progresses. One of the ways this is assessed is how well the elder can perform ADLs and IADLs.

ADLs include being able to transfer (getting oneself from a lying to a sitting position and from a sitting to a standing position), walking, toileting oneself, bathing, dressing, and eating.

IADLs include housekeeping, use of phone, bill paying and managing financial matters, getting groceries, laundry, food preparation, transportation, and taking medication correctly.

If elders are unable to do just one of the ADLs, they need assistance. It may be they just need some adaptive equipment like a cane or walker to perform the ADL, but they *do* need some aid or help.

These standard definitions are used in a variety of ways. Long term care insurance companies base their reimbursement on whether an elder is unable to do one or more of these activities. Discharge planners in a hospital base their discharge plans on whether patients can perform these tasks. Medical equipment needs are based on the assessment of ADLs and IADLs.

Online you will find DME suppliers in your area by simply entering DME in a web search engine like Google, Yahoo, or Bing. You can also ask your local drugstore for the nearest DME company, although some drugstores supply a variety of such equipment and will bill Medicare for you. Not all DME supplies are covered by Medicare, and you will need a physician's order to bill Medicare.

ALARM MECHANISMS TO ASSURE SAFETY

There are also various alarm mechanisms to assure safety. One common alarm is something that looks like a watch or a necklace. The elder wears this device 24/7, and if a fall occurs, the elder pushes the button on the device and it signals an alarm in a staffed setting who then sends help to the elder. These can be a great device but only under certain conditions. These devices can only be used if:

■ The elder is committed to wearing the device at all times even in the shower and when sleeping.

■ The elder must be able to remember to push the button if a fall occurs.

In other words, these devices are not helpful if the elder has short-term memory issues or dementia or refuses to wear the device. Many families buy these devices and pay for the monthly service only to find the elder does not wear the device or when something happens, fails to push the button. It can give a family or caregivers a false sense of security. This does not mean these devices are not useful, but you must assess whether it is realistic for these devices to work in your individual circumstances.

There are also chair and bed alarms for caregivers to know if an elder is getting out of a chair or bed. There are alarms that signal it is time to take medications. Medication alarms that cue an elder to take their medication can give the same false sense of security as the watch or necklace alarm. An alarm may tell the elder to take a particular medication and actually dispense the medication into a cup, but if the elder is hard of hearing or has short-term memory loss, they are not effective. An elder may hear the alarm stating it is time to take the medication, but in the time it takes to walk across the room, the elder may have forgotten what to do. This causes untold frustration on the part of the family, as they think they have found the solution to a particular problem, but it does not work. Understanding what will and will not work sometimes takes the assessment and advice of a professional such as a care manager or home care nurse.

SAFETY CHECKLIST

Here is a room-by-room checklist from experiences and many sources over the years.

KITCHEN

◖ Have all commonly used items stored at convenient height so you do not have to use a chair or step stool.

◖ Clean up spills immediately.

◖ Use an electric teapot with a shut off mechanism when water boils.

◖ Do not wear flowing sleeved bathrobes or night wear in kitchen as it can catch on fire.

◖ Avoid grease fires by keeping stove and oven clean.

◖ Remove throw rugs and any clutter on floor or counters.

◖ Install adequate lighting over work surfaces.

◖ Keep an ABC fire extinguisher within reach (usually kept under the sink).

◖ Have a phone with emergency numbers nearby.

◖ Empty old or expired food frequently from the refrigerator to prevent food-borne illnesses.

◖ Assess need for adaptive aids such as reachers, or large-handled utensils.

◖ Do not use stove or oven for warmth!

◖ Install a smoke alarm near the kitchen.

BATHROOM

◖ Place non-skid adhesive strips on shower/bath floor.

◖ Have non-skid mat on floor beside shower/bath.

◖ Regulate the hot-water temperature no more than 110 (some say 120) degrees.

◖ Assess for bath bench or shower chair if needed to sit down while bathing.

◖ Install a hand-held shower head.

◖ Place grab bars for the toilet and tub. Hire a contractor or handy person to do this for you.

◖ Use a toilet raiser if needed to help get on and off the toilet.

◖ Do NOT use bath oils or any liquid that causes the shower/tub surface to become slippery.

◖ Install automatic night-lights in bathroom.

◖ Store electrical items as hair dryers and razors away from water source. Unplug when not using.

◀ Have the pathway to the bathroom clear of all clutter and throw rugs.

BEDROOM

◀ Install a smoke alarm near the bedroom.

◀ Bed needs to be the correct height — low enough to sit on but not too low that it makes getting up difficult.

◀ Have a path to bathroom uncluttered with no throw rugs or consider a bedside commode or urinal for nighttime use.

◀ Use a bed-assist aid if you need help getting out of bed.

◀ Have a bedside table with flashlight, phone, and lamp.

◀ Have slippers nearby but not in pathway.

◀ DO NOT SMOKE IN BED. Smoking in bed plus sleep medications are a recipe for disaster!

TELEPHONE

◀ Assess the need for magnified dials and the need for louder rings and sound.

◀ Arrange for daily check-in calls.

◀ Have the phone programmed for commonly used calls or have a list by the phone to call for help.

◀ At a minimum, have a phone in the kitchen and bedroom, but also consider an additional phone in the living room/TV room. Cell phones that stay on an elder's person may work for those who can remember to charge the battery daily. You do not want to be hurrying to answer the phone.

GENERAL GUIDELINES FOR ALL ROOMS

◀ Install adequate lighting (100 watts or higher).

◀ Remove all throw or scatter rugs.

◀ Tape or nail down all loose carpeting and linoleum.

◀ Remove all obstacles from pathways.

◀ Do not overload electrical sockets.

◀ Place commonly used items within reach.

◀ Have a disaster plan and disaster kit especially if the elder is on oxygen or other electronic medical devices.

◀ Wear non-slip low-heeled shoes that fit well. Stocking feet cause slips.

◀ Remember to have a consistent date to test and change batteries on smoke alarms.

◀ Be alert to pets and children who may run in your pathway.

◀ Use assistive devices like canes, walking sticks, or walkers if needed or when on uneven surfaces.

STAIRS

◀ Since most falls occur on the top or bottom step, paint these two steps or place brightly colored tape on the edge of these stairs.

◀ Install handrails on both sides of stairs/steps.

◀ Install adequate light at top and bottom of stairs.

◀ Do not pile stuff on steps.

- Install non-skid rubber or vinyl treads on bare stairs.
- Always leave one hand free to use rails.

OUTSIDE

- Repair any uneven walks or steps.
- Have rails on both sides of steps.
- Make sure all exit routes to the outside are in working order and free of obstacles.
- Keep pathways free of shrubs, debris, roots, etc.
- If you live in a place with snowy or icy conditions, consider painting outside steps with sand for better traction. You can also buy Yaktrax to put on shoes in icy conditions.
- Keep the outside clear of snow and ice.
- Have ramps built if outside stairs become a hazard.

DEMENTIA SAFETY

- Do not rush or hurry.
- Put gates or barriers at the top of the stairs.
- Remove any electrical devices that could burn the elder, such as heaters.
- Use safety covers on doorknobs or door alarms so you know if the elder is trying to wander.
- If the elder is confused, you may have to disable the stove and oven and just use a microwave.
- Remove any sharp objects like knives, razors, etc.

◀ Remove any guns.

◀ Keep medications in a lock box.

◀ Register elder in a wandering program.

◀ Keep a recent photo of the elder.

◀ Do not leave a demented elder alone, especially if he/she cannot respond to an emergency.

TASK LIST

☐ COMPLETE THE HOME SAFETY CHECKLIST AND MAKE CHANGES BEFORE AN ACCIDENT OR FALL OCCURS.

☐ HAVE ANY FALL EVALUATED BY YOUR PHYSICIAN AND FIX THE CAUSE.

"If I'd known I was gonna live this long, I would have taken better care of myself."
■ UBIE BLAKE AT 100 YEARS OF AGE

CHAPTER FOUR

MEDICAL CARE AND MEDICATIONS

In this Chapter...

■ WHO IS ON YOUR HEALTH TEAM

■ RESPONSIBILITIES FOR THE MD OFFICE VISIT

■ YOUR DOCTOR OFFICE VISIT

■ MEDICATION COMPLIANCE

WHO IS ON YOUR HEALTH CARE TEAM

If you have been following the plan, you now have an advocate or several advocates who know your wishes, all your paper work/documentation is complete, including your personal health record, and your living environment is as safe as possible. This chapter is a discussion about your medical care and medications. This chapter does not go into specific disease conditions, but rather covers basic health care needed by all elders. It also covers problems and issues elders face regarding their medical care as they age.

Establish yourself with a primary care physician who will see you for most of your medical needs. If possible, find a geriatrician (an MD who specializes in the conditions and care of the elderly.) Your primary care physician will refer you to a specialist only if necessary. Even if you have no specialists on board, you will still need a team:

◀ Primary care physician

◀ Eye doctor

◀ Dentist

◀ Podiatrist (foot doctor)

When elders are initially seen by a care manager and are asked who these vital four team members are, it is not unusual to get a blank stare.

"Oh, I have not seen my dentist for years. In fact, I think he died."

"I don't need a dentist! I am too old for that."

"Primary care physician? You mean Doc Jones? He retired some years back, and I have just not found another one."

"Eye doctor! These old eyes — there is not anything to be done about them."

OUTCOMES OF NEGLECTED HEALTH ISSUES

Neglect of eye health can lead to quality of life issues and safety issues. And then there are the teeth and feet! Teeth (mouth care) and feet are the most neglected parts of an elder's body. It is not unusual to find an elder's feet with chronic fungus, overgrown toenails sometimes literally curling over the ends of the toes, and other minor infections. This can affect mobility as well as lead to major infections.

Teeth are so important for an elder's health as they assist in the chewing of food thus largely contributing to good nutrition. If you have poor or painful teeth, ingestion of food decreases. If teeth have been neglected over time, the chances are very good that gum disease is present, which endangers not only the teeth but also cardiac health. False teeth are a poor substitute for one's own teeth.

ADDITIONAL SPECIALISTS

In addition to the four essential health team members, elders may have a plethora of other physicians. The list can be endless: a cardiologist for heart issues, a GI (gastroenterologist) for any problems with the digestive tract, a pulmonologist and/or an allergist for chronic respiratory issues, an endocrinologist for endocrine issues such as diabetes, an oncologist for cancer illnesses, an orthopedist for bone and joint problems, a neurologist for memory deficits and dementia issues. You can have as many as eight physicians and specialists all involved in your health. This train often runs off the track, as physicians are notorious for not talking to each other resulting in duplicate tests, treatments, and medications. In all fairness, this is not just the fault of multiple physicians, as you will see in the following example.

A long-distance daughter requested that I see her mother for an assessment and medication management. The mother was not feeling well but was very vague about her symptoms. After getting all the necessary paperwork out of the way, I then asked her to bring me all her medications that were in the house. She emerged with two shoeboxes overflowing with bottles of medications — some over the counter but mostly prescriptions. (Polypharmacy, the use of multiple medications, is an enormous problem in this country.) Many of her medications were out of date, and I convinced her to place these in a paper bag so I could take them to a disposal center.

We finally got the current medications lined up. This woman liked to *doctor hop*, which means she often sought several doctors' assistance for a single problem. If she could not get what she thought she needed from one doctor, she went to another until she obtained what she wanted. As I got the current bottles lined up, I noticed that she had several bottles of varying strengths of digoxin, a cardiac medication. I asked her if she was taking all of the bottles, and she stated she was. Her presenting symptoms resembled those of digoxin toxicity. In addition, she was taking large doses of a water pill or diuretic. With a large dose of diuretic, potassium may also be ordered to counteract the loss of potassium when on a diuretic. The potassium bottle was present, but was empty. It turns out, she had sought digoxin from several doctors without telling them she was already on a digoxin dose from another doctor. She was short of money, so did not feel she needed to continue with potassium once it was gone as "it is only a vitamin." She did not know that potassium is one of the most important ions in the body with several vital functions. This woman was not only in digoxin toxicity but her potassium was dangerously low.

This example illustrates the need for the updated personal health record to be present at all appointments with your health care providers along with an advocate. It is not the physician's responsibility to take hours to figure out what medications you are taking and which ones you have decided to stop taking.

RESPONSIBILITIES FOR THE MD OFFICE VISIT

You, the elder or your advocate, must take some responsibility for your medications. Go to a physician's office prepared. When the physician asks what medications you are taking, avoid saying, "Oh I take that little pink pill and then there is a large white one which I take at night." This means nothing to the physician or the pharmacist. This is the reason for the personal health record, which is your responsibility to keep up-to-date with your medication regime, date each medicine was ordered, the physician who ordered it, dosage, and why it was ordered. (See "Documentation" on page 21.) Eventually the electronic medical record may eliminate some of these issues, but until then, you and/or your advocate must be proactive in keeping your medication list accurate and current.

BASIC APPOINTMENTS, VACCINES, TESTS

Keep regularly scheduled appointments with your various physicians. The following is a list of very basic appointments, vaccines, and tests to do on a regular scheduled time frame:

❶ Dental appointments every six months for cleaning and finding problems early.

❷ Podiatry appointments every two to four months or as needed for nail trimming and foot issues.

❸ Primary care physician as needed but always every six to twelve months.

❹ Eye appointments yearly or as needed.

❺ GU (genito-urinary) physician for men and gynecologist for women yearly for prostate check and pap test. Sometimes your primary care physician can do these simple tests as well.

❻ Mammograms yearly for women.

❼ Colonoscopy every 5 years.

❽ Shots:

◀ Flu shots yearly.

◀ Pneumonia shot. Check with your doctor.

◀ Shingles shot. Check with your doctor.

◀ Tetanus shot every 10 years. Sometimes tetanus is combined with dyptheria and called TD. Tetanus may also be combined with pertussis (whooping cough) and called TDAP. Consult your physician as to which immunization you need.

◀ Varicella (chickenpox). Check with your doctor. Needed if you have never had chickenpox or have never received the vaccine.

Your doctor may order blood work on an as-needed basis.

YOUR DOCTOR OFFICE VISIT

Whenever you visit any of your medical providers, take your updated personal health record and any insurance cards with you, even if you think they already have all your information.

Under the Medicare system, your doctor is only paid for a certain number of minutes per visit. Be prepared to hand your personal health record to the physician or their assistant who may be taking the information, but also have your questions, issues, or reason for the visit briefly written out.

Accompanying a recent patient to the doctor's office, it was surprising to see a sign in the exam room stating, "Your doctor has time for only one question. If you have more questions, please make another appointment." Although I dislike this process, I can understand the reason for it under the present system.

Take an advocate with you when you go to the doctor's office. Most doctors no longer have the time to visit with their patients. They may give a lot of information in a short amount of time. Sometimes this information is given to you in a printed form, but this may not always be the case. It always helps to have another person write down what the doctor says. If the doctor is notifying you of a serious condition, it is even more important to have your advocate with you to help absorb the information, as you may be overwhelmed by what you are hearing.

Recently I had both of my knees replaced. The doctor had most of the information written down in a three ring binder for me to take home. Being a little nervous about all the information, I was very appreciative of the binder, which I could read at my leisure at home. There was also an informational meeting at the hospital, which was attended by both my adult daughter and me. Although I took notes, she also gleaned information that I had missed. Having another set of eyes and ears just helps to prevent things from sliding or being missed.

If your physician is prescribing a new medication, you need to ask why you should take this medication, what are the benefits and risks/side effects, how much (dose) and how often, how long do you take it (duration), and are there any alternatives other than medicating, or is there a generic that is just as effective. Speak up and make sure you understand what the physician is telling you.

The completed doctor office visit is just the beginning. You need to process the information and carry out any orders or instructions. Either you and/or your advocate need to be sure that the necessary prescriptions are taken to the pharmacy and filled. Other doctor orders such as the need for physical therapy need to be scheduled. Specific lifestyle changes the doctor ordered such as the need for exercise, nutritional changes, weight loss, smoking cessation, alcohol reduction, need to be discussed and a plan drawn up for implementation. Your doctor may have ordered some tests or for you to see another specialist. All these items need prompt follow up, scheduling, and planning.

An advocate and/or care manager usually accompanies elders to their doctors' appointments, and makes sure that their personal health record including their medication list is complete and up to date. Questions have been discussed with the elder ahead of time and a written question list is handed to the doctor when entering the office. The advocate and/or care manager takes notes during the visit and asks for clarification on any information the doctor provides. The advocate and/or care manager then makes sure that all orders and/or instructions are carried out as soon as possible and discusses the findings with the elder. Notification of appropriate family members is provided with the information from the doctor office visit.

FINDING A NEW PRIMARY CARE PHYSICIAN

From experience, one of the best ways to find a primary care physician is by word of mouth. Ask everyone and anyone you know who their doctor is and how they like her or him. If you belong to a faith community, ask the faith leader or other members of the faith community. Ask your pharmacist or a nurse in the community. If you see specialists, ask them whom they would recommend. Ask your dentist. Ask your neighbor. Ask the person ahead of you in line. Eventually you will find that a couple of names will keep rising to the top. Keep in mind also the location of this doctor. Draw a five or ten-mile perimeter around your home base and try to find a doctor in that vicinity. Many patients avoid going to the doctor as "it is just too far."

Another way to find a physician is to use the computer. Look up a particular physician or request a search of internists in your geographical area. You will come up with a list. You can then look at each physician's site and also look at patient comments about a particular physician. Usually the physician credentials are listed under their name. Some people do not care, but it is good to know where they went to college, what medical school they attended, where they did their residency, and what special training they have had.

There are some areas of the country that have what is called a *geriatrician*. This is a physician who has specialized in care of the elderly patient. There are not nearly enough of them to meet the need, but if you are lucky enough to have one in your area, it would be worth investigating this individual.

Finding a doctor is just not about credentials and training, however. You and your doctor will hopefully form a bond and trust over time. You both have to feel comfortable working with each other. After you have done a search, make an appointment with the chosen doctor. Make sure when you call for an appointment that the physician takes new Medicare patients. Take your personal health record with you and preferably your advocate as well. This initial visit is longer than routine visits and is reimbursed as such. Have a list of questions written out before the visit.

You may want to ask at what hospital the physician has privileges. Some physicians may not have privileges at the hospital you prefer. You may want to know if they, on special occasions, make house calls. You may want to know if they have an email system where patients can email their concerns. Email can be a powerful tool for staying in contact with each other and getting your questions/concerns answered in a timely manner. Also ask who covers for them when they are away?

At this initial visit, the physician is evaluating you, but you are also evaluating the physician. When you enter the office, be aware of the office staff. Do they seem distracted and unhelpful? Is the medical assistant who may do the initial vital signs competent and helpful? Is the physician a good listener? Does he/she value what you are telling them, or are they somewhat dismissive of your concerns? Be aware of any gut feelings either positive or negative. Are they in a hurry and seem distracted? Do they honor your questions? Do you have a feeling of comfort and trust during the appointment?

After the appointment, discuss the experience with your advocate and elicit how the advocate felt during the appointment. If you went alone, sit quietly and assess your own feelings. This will be an important relationship, and if possible, you want to get it right. Clearly, if it was not a good experience, you will continue your search.

EVALUATING YOUR DOCTOR

When patients complain about their doctors, it usually goes like this.

"My doctor just does not have time for me."

"He/she never returns my calls."

"I need an appointment soon, and the doctor cannot see me for the next three months."

Then there is the other side of the story when I speak to physicians.

"Oh, Mrs. Jones? The reason I do not always call her back is she calls five or six times a day with various needs."

"Mr. Smith does have an appointment for next week, plus I just saw him last week."

I have learned the hard way that when I *assume,* it often makes an "ass" out of "u" and "me." After doing a thorough check to verify the stories and finding that perhaps the particular physician in question is not attentive to this particular patient, I will advise the patient to consider another doctor. I use the example of the car mechanic by asking the elder what she would do if she took her car to the mechanic who charged $1000 to fix the vehicle. The vehicle falls apart a few days later. The elder usually replies that the mechanic would get a piece of her mind plus the return of the $1000 AND she would find a new mechanic. Elders are usually very adamant and passionate about this scenario. I then ask if their body isn't more valuable than their car.

For whatever the reason, it is very difficult for patients to confront their doctors if they feel their needs are not being met. I will always suggest that patients meet with their physicians and explain what the issues are. Often doctors are unaware of how the patient feels and are more than willing to rectify the situation. That being said, if no common ground can be found between the doctor and the elder, then the elder and/or the advocate need to search for another doctor and request that all records from the former doctor be sent to the new doctor. This can be done over the phone and does not need to be a big deal.

Before you decide to leave your doctor, make sure you have a new one on board who is willing to accept you into the practice and who will take new Medicare patients. In some parts of the country, doctors who accept new Medicare patients into their practices are few and far between. **Do not get rid of a doctor who may not be your ideal, but is usually adequate for your needs until you are sure you have another.**

MEDICATION COMPLIANCE

Medication issues are one of the biggest reasons for unsatisfactory medical outcomes. We are an impatient culture, and we have great faith in the science of medications and their ability to cure immediately. Many elders gradually fall into a morass of complex medication regimes, called polypharmacy, where they may be taking ten, fifteen, or twenty-plus medications a day. (This includes both over-the-counters and vitamin supplements.) Since many elders do not want to throw away any medications, they may often go back and start taking a medication from several years ago thinking it may help whatever complaint they have presently.

Often a physician may have no clue what a patient is actually taking or not taking, as patients may often pick and choose what to take as in the example of the woman not taking her potassium. This can cause some dangerous drug interactions. Patients will often take the medications they can afford and simply not fill the more expensive ones. Short-term memory loss and dementia may also compound this issue as the elder cannot remember the medications to take and when. This is often when adult children get involved, as they gradually realize mom or dad is not managing medications correctly. If the patient is seeing multiple doctors or *doctor hopping,* the medication regime can get impossibly tangled and the outcome can be disastrous.

One such common drug interaction is when an elder is placed on the blood thinner, Coumadin (warfarin). If an elder is stable on Coumadin and then decides to take an aspirin, a serious bleeding episode may occur as aspirin increases the blood thinning ability of Coumadin. Some of the drug interactions are extremely complex and presenting symptoms may lead to many tests trying to pinpoint the cause.

Just to give you an idea of how much this costs on a national basis, here are some statistics on this issue. Among older adults, forty percent of hospital admissions are due to medication-related issues. This translates to higher costs nationwide and poor outcomes for the elder. According to the World Health Organization (WHO), in 2003, only fifty percent of patients with chronic conditions in developed countries adhere to their treatment recommendations.[1]

Knowing the risk factors for something bad to happen regarding medication regimes can lead to prevention. Risks are as follows:

Number of medications taken. The more medications ingested, including over-the-counter (OTCs), and vitamin/herbals, the more likelihood the drug interaction. The magic number seems to be ten. The more medications taken over the number ten, the more likelihood of at least one interaction.[2]

Types of medications taken. Certain classes of drugs commonly prescribed to the elderly increase the incidence of interactions. These are blood thinners, high blood pressure medications, medications for depression and for sleeping.

Expired medications. Throw away old or expired medications. Ask your pharmacist about ways to dispose of medications so they do not harm our environment.

Multiple physicians.

Changes in how the aging body metabolizes medications. These include changes in our kidneys and liver as we age that impact how the medication is metabolized and/or excreted.

Interactions with vitamins, herbals, supplements.

Interactions with alcohol consumption.

Multiple diagnoses of chronic conditions necessitating more medications for each condition.

One of the best ways to prevent the risk of drug interactions is to purchase all medications from one pharmacy. Many elders buy their medications from multiple pharmacies based on the cost savings. This means that the pharmacist may not have a record of all the drugs you may be taking and therefore cannot warn or advise you on medication interactions in your drug profile.

If an elder is visiting multiple physicians, it is again imperative to take a copy of your complete, updated medication list to each office visit. Ask your physicians if the medication regime can be simplified.

It is important for the elder or advocate to read any labels or materials that will come with your medication. The same goes for OTCs and any supplements. One can always use the Internet for information on drug interactions.

Care managers play an extremely important role in this issue often spending hours sorting out a complex medication regime, contacting various physicians, getting all medications from one pharmacy, and organizing the medications in such a way so the elder is taking the regime appropriately and accurately.

TAKING MEDICATIONS CORRECTLY

There have been many ways devised over time to enable the elder to take their medications correctly. Care managers have probably tried them all. In speaking with the elder and/or their advocates, most people just desperately want to try anything.

"Should I call my parents twice a day to remind them to take their medications?"

"Should I send a neighbor over to the house daily to give them their medications?"

On more than one occasion a neighbor assigned by the family to manage a med regime has taken it upon himself to decide what medications the elder should take, leaving some out and adding others! When confronted why he was doing this, the neighbor replied, "Oh, he does not need that medication. My wife took that and it made her sick." As you can see, the best plans can slide downhill without supervision or oversight.

The main issue when there is poor compliance with a medication regime is to discover the cause. Is the elder suffering from short-term memory loss or some form of dementia? Is there a vision or hearing problem? Is there poor manual dexterity in getting the bottle open and feeling the pill in their hand? Is the elder denying the reality of their chronic condition thus refusing to follow instructions? It is important to assess why the issue is happening.

For instance, it makes no sense to buy a recording device telling the elder it is time to take medicine, if the elder is deaf. These types of devices may remind the elder or you may call the elder to remind him, but if the elder has short-term memory loss, he may forget why you called as soon as he hangs up the phone. The elder may hear the reminder, but as soon as he walks across the room to his medications, he may have forgotten what he is supposed to do. The elder may start a medication, but then after a few days, does not "feel right" and refuses to take the medication any longer, attributing symptoms to the new medication.

In short, if the elder has significant memory loss or other dementia symptoms, you can try all the gadgets and gizmos in the world, and you will still be on a slippery slope. About the only way to have reliable compliance in this instance is to have a caregiver, an advocate, or family member personally administer the medications on site. This can be costly at most and inconvenient at the least, but this may be the only way to assure the medications are taken correctly.

There are many gadgets on the market to assist the elder with their medications. The following is a brief list:

Mediplanner. This is a plastic rectangular box with small-lidded compartments. Each compartment is labeled with the day of the week. You can get a mediplanner for the AM and one for the PM and label them as such. Or you can get a mediplanner that is much larger and has rows of compartments for various times of the day: A.M., LUNCH, P.M., BEDTIME. This does cover most regime times. Either the elder, if able, or the advocates fill the mediplanner once a week and oversee the compliance by checking to see if the appropriate day and time is emptied or not. This works well for many and is an inexpensive option. Care managers may also fill mediplanners and instruct advocates or caregivers to give reminders.

Packaging medications. You may ask the pharmacist to *bubble pack* the medications in one of several ways. This is an 8 x 11-inch piece of cardboard with thirty-one bubbles on it. The pharmacist peels off a backing on each bubble and fills the bubble with the appropriate medications. The pharmacist can either use one card per medication in which case you will have multiple cards or the pharmacist can fill the bubble with all the meds to be taken in the AM for the thirty-one days. This method, called the *salad pack*, as there are different medications in the bubble, is what I prefer as a care manager. It is just easier for the elder or the caregiver to push out one bubble rather than multiple bubbles. This service does add a cost to the medications usually three or four dollars per refill of the bubbles. Voluntary caregivers also appreciate not having to fill mediplanners with multiple meds, thus decreasing the risk of errors. There still needs to be an advocate who checks the bubble packs. I had several experiences where I would count the pills in the bubble and found the pharmacist had missed a pill. Medicine is an intensive human labor issue and human beings all make mistakes. Constant vigilance is necessary.

Reminding devices. Googling medication reminding devices, 75,400 results appeared! These all fall within several categories — various alarms and recorded reminders either to be set up in a room or to be worn on the person in the form of a watch. Some actually dispense the medication when the alarm sounds. Again these may work for some and not for others depending on the elder's abilities.

Use of on-site non-skilled caregivers either hired or voluntary. Hiring a caregiver either privately or through an agency is probably one of the most expensive methods but also the most effective. Many agencies offer what are called *medication visits* at anywhere from $30.00 to $60.00 per visit to actually assist with the medications. The visits usually last one to two hours and may include other household tasks. Most agency non-skilled caregivers are not allowed to actually pour meds from a bottle into the elder's hand or fill mediplanners, due to state regulations. The provisions of these regulations can vary from state to state. This means that someone else must fill the mediplanner weekly, either a skilled nurse (RN, LVN) or an advocate the elder or family has designated. Bubble packs do make this easier as the pharmacist has already filled medications into a bubble pack.

Use of elder's systems. From experience, many elders living independently in their homes are very proud of their particular system to remember their medication regime. Some of these systems are very creative. Many elders have established a routine to take specific medications with meals and lay the medications out accordingly in cups, egg cartons, various bowls, jewelry box compartments, baskets etc. You name it, and it is being used. Do not try to fix what is not broken. If their system seems to be working, leave it alone.

TASK LIST

☐   ESTABLISH YOUR HEALTH TEAM — PRIMARY CARE
     PHYSICIAN, DENTIST, PODIATRIST, AND EYE DOCTOR.

☐   TAKE YOUR PHR AND WRITTEN QUESTIONS TO EVERY
     HEALTH PROVIDER.

☐   MAKE AND KEEP YOUR ROUTINE APPOINTMENTS, AND
     FOLLOW UP ON ALL PHYSICIAN ORDERS.

☐   DEVISE A SYSTEM FOR TAKING MEDICATIONS CORRECTLY.

*"We turn not older with years
but newer every day."*
■ EMILY DICKINSON

LEADING A MEANINGFUL LIFE

Quality of life is a broad topic and involves those aspects of our lives that give our lives meaning, satisfaction, and fulfillment. They may be a reason to get up in the morning. It may be a passion for excellence in a sport such as golf or passion for a creative pursuit as painting or gardening. It may be giving your time as a volunteer to a worthy cause or helping with grandchildren. These pursuits may be things you longed to do all your life, but never found time when working and/or raising a family. One of the biggest aspects for quality of life is socialization or relationships. As human beings, we are social beings, and we tend not to do well when we are isolated from relationships with others including our pets.

Why are these issues so peculiarly important to the elder population? One reason is the elder's world shrinks, as mobility is impaired due to vision and hearing deficits. Driving may become difficult or nonexistent. Energies are limited, and thus, time out of the home is decreased. Depression plays a big part of elders being shut in. The elder just does not feel up to seeing people when depressed. Death of a long-term partner or spouse can cause a shutdown in social activities for the remaining person, as she does not feel comfortable venturing out on her own. Certain symptoms and/or diseases may cause a cessation of social interactions. Loss of long-term friendships can be especially debilitating. All of these reasons lead to an isolation of the elder that only increases her sense of loneliness and abandonment and exacerbates her depression.

The emphasis in our culture on independence makes it hard for the elder person to reach out and ask for help.

Thus, we find many elders living lives of loneliness and de-spair due to isolation. We used to live in villages and towns where everyone knew everyone else, and elders spent their older years living with adult children, other relatives, or being looked after by the village. Although this may still happen today, many elders may be estranged from their children, or the adult children are unable to support an el-der on a daily basis due to distance or other factors. There are many cases where the only contact an elder may have with the outside world is the Meals on Wheels volunteer once or twice a week. This is not a sustainable lifestyle, and many elders decline quickly under these circumstances.

SYMPTOMS OF A DECLINING QUALITY OF LIFE

What are the symptoms that the quality of life is declin-ing for the elder?

■ There is a sudden or gradual decline in doing the things that have brought joy to the elder. This can be something as simple as not wanting to cook after enjoying cooking for a lifetime, or no longer enjoying gardening, which she always wanted to perfect. He may no longer want to join his friends in the weekly golf game or the weekly bridge game. She may no longer find joy in her grandchildren.

■ The elder is no longer interested in engaging with friends and rebuffs efforts to continue the friendship.

■ The elder may no longer be willing to travel to see children and grandchildren or go on outings.

■ The elder may not communicate by phone, email, or mail.

- ■ The elder is not interested in exercise or physical activity.

- ■ Decreased appetite may be causing weight loss.

- ■ Feelings of boredom or hopelessness may be expressed. "What have I got to live for?"

- ■ The elder may have paralyzing fears — fear of falling, fear of an incontinent accident, fear of going out alone after losing a spouse, fear of failing, fears around death and dying.

- ■ The elder may no longer have an interest in his/her appearance and grooming.

- ■ The elder may be resistant to any kind of help or assistance.

Some of you may be thinking that these are all symptoms of depression. The answer is yes and no. They may indicate signs of depression or signs of grief. An elder who has just lost his life partner of fifty or sixty years may be in a legitimate stage of grief and these symptoms are normal after such a loss. The difference between being in a state of sadness (thus exhibiting some of these symptoms) and depression is the length of time a person remains in these stages and the severity of the symptoms.

STORY: LOSS OF A SPOUSE

 My own mother is a perfect example of this. My mother lost her husband after nearly sixty years of marriage. After helping her with the funeral and closing my Dad's estate for several weeks, I went home to California to resume my life and work. I kept in close phone contact with my mother and spent many hours on the phone listening to her grief and lending whatever support I could. She sounded sad on the phone, but I expected her to sound sad. Three months after the death of her husband, she fell breaking all her ribs on one side while hurrying to the bathroom in the middle of the night. She had lost thirty pounds and had worn out her advocates who could no longer care for her needs. She needed to be hospitalized for her acute depression, secondary to her loss of her spouse. My mother's grief over the loss of her spouse simply swamped the ship.

In spite of counselors, psychiatrists, pastors, and medications, her grief over time did not subside. (This is one of the differences between an episode of sadness and depression.) My brother and I brought her to live near us, but she never recouped. She lived another six years in a sort of limbo, not really caring what happened to her or to those around her. It was a difficult time for all of us, as we loved her and wanted to see her regain some of her former happiness for her family, friends, and activities.

Although frustrating at times for my brother and me, we both came to the conclusion that all we could do was love her just the way she was at that time. Even now, after fourteen years since her death, I feel a deep sadness that somehow she never could find enjoyment in life during those last six years in spite of everyone's best efforts.

This is when the *Journey through Old* can become tough and difficult for everyone involved. But then, no one ever said journeys would always have sunny weather with no rain or storms along the way or straight even paths on which to tread.

STAYING ENGAGED

So how do we tread through this *Journey through Old* with all its losses and changes?

The Centenarian Studies (The New England Centenarian Study),[1] which are studies of elders who have reached one hundred years of age, have found some interesting things about surviving the first hundred years.

These are people who have had losses! Many have lost a devoted spouse, and some have lost children. After all, if one lives to be one hundred, their children could be in their eighties. I have had a few very aged clients, one hundred or over, who have lost one or more elder children. Although I, myself, can think of nothing more devastating, I was in awe of these people who did go on to live productive, interesting, and yes, joyful lives. The Centenarian Study and other studies found that there were consistent themes running through the lives of these survivors:

- They had a burning passion or interest that they looked forward to each day, a reason to get out of bed in the morning.

- They had a spiritual pathway of some kind. They believed in a higher power and practiced their pathway with regularity.

- They had a love of music. They either played an instrument or had a passion for music in some form.

- They kept themselves in shape. Their exercise included strength training. They ate correctly and maintained an appropriate weight. Smoking was rare and alcohol use was small.

■ They had a social network and maintained that network. They did not isolate themselves, but sought out and found joy in the company of others.

■ They had the capacity to bounce back quickly from grief and losses. This does not mean they do not experience grief, but the time spent in this state is reasonable. It does not swamp the ship. They get back to their activities and friends within a reasonable time.

This is not to say that all people who live to be one hundred are well and healthy. Only about twenty-five percent are alert and healthy, but it is useful to know what contributes to a healthy and abundant life well into the *Journey through Old*. In this case, knowledge is truly wealth on a number of levels. Genetics of course play a part. Longevity runs in families.

WHAT DO YOU DO IF LIFE HAS LOST ITS MEANING

What do you do as an elder if you feel life has lost its meaning and staying at home is no longer an option? What do adult children do if they notice a decline in their loved one's quality of life?

First, do an assessment and try to find the reason for the decline. It may be perfectly obvious in some situations as the recent loss of a devoted spouse or partner, the loss of sight, hearing, or the loss of abilities to enjoy lifetime passions. It also may be far subtler or just be a gradual decline for no apparent reason.

The first step in an assessment is to consult your primary care physician about a physical reason for this decline. Medications, side effects, and medication interactions can often produce some of these symptoms. Your physician may also do a short questionnaire to assess for depression. For grief after a significant loss, a grief counselor and/or support group may be appropriate. Your doctor might suggest a neurological assessment if signs and symptoms of dementia or short-term memory loss are present. The idea is to rule out any medical reason for the decline.

Second, attempt to make sure that a social network is either re-established or new ones found. Senior centers can sometimes be literal lifesavers in these situations, and they have group support for many of life's hard issues for this *Journey through Old*. (See "Senior Centers" on page 120 for more information about senior centers.)

For those of you who do not have attentive children nearby, or for adult children, who for whatever reason are unable to provide support, there are steps you can take. The quality of care and attention needed often depends on the elder's or family's resources available. (Medicare does not pay for this type of care.)

DECIDING TO HAVE CARE AT HOME

First, let's look at the best-case scenario which would require private resources. Let's say you are an attentive, long-distance adult child who is the first to notice a parent's decline. Of course, the best scenario is the elder notices he/she needs help and takes action, but let's assume the adult child is the first to notice.

Have a conversation with your loved one, ideally face to face. Explain what you are observing and ask her what she is feeling about her circumstance. The usual reaction from the elder is denial. "Well, don't worry about me! I am doing just fine and furthermore, I do not need any help." There are many renditions of this mantra, some long and some short, as "Hell no, I do not need help!" Remember the lesson of the prince in the Tolstoy story and that cornerstone of our country, *independence*. We are all terrified of losing our independence, so expect some resistance.

Have a conversation with other family members, usually siblings. It is important for all family members to be on the same sheet of music. In family conferences some siblings may feel help or intervention is needed but others do not. Some will be astounded how much this help is going to cost. The adult child who lives nearest the elder may feel impending doom knowing that much of this care needed may fall on their shoulders. Others may feel the cost of such care is going to deplete resources they were counting on in the future, thus causing resentment toward the elder. All of these issues need to be ironed out before confronting a resisting elder.

Contact a care manager. Call an elder care manager in your area to assist you as you begin this journey. When issues between family members or between the family and the elder seem at an impasse, a care manager, as a calm, outside, objective voice, can mediate the impasse into a positive outcome for all. Some care managers even specialize in conflict resolution regarding care for an elder. They have experience in these circumstances and can help you and the elder make this transition. Sometimes having an outside expert speak with your elder rather than a family member can have very positive outcomes. Elder care managers work in a variety of ways. Some are associated with elder care attorneys and come as part of the services the attorney offers if managing an estate. They also may be associated with an elder care agency, which provides non-skilled caregivers in the home. Generally, they work on their own, and may charge from $60.00 to $120.00 an hour depending on where in the country they work.

Take it slowly. If there is resistance, start with small steps when possible. An elder care manager or you, the adult child, can start researching resources in the elder's community that provide assistance. This assistance is usually in the form of a non-skilled caregiver coming into the home for what is called personal care defined as bathing, dressing, meal preparation, transportation to the grocery store and appointments, and light housekeeping (vacuuming, laundry, dusting, pet care, emptying trash, making or changing the bed, keeping the bathroom and kitchen clean). A non-skilled caregiver means someone who has had some training in the field of personal care. Certified nursing assistants have completed a course of study and have passed an exam attesting to their knowledge of these skills. Non-skilled also means that the care required does NOT require the skills of a registered nurse or physical therapist.

How does one find a caregiver that will give quality care in the elder's home and how much does it cost? The ideal way is to go through an agency that specializes in this type of care. Your elder care manager will know who to call or can make the arrangements for you. If you are not using an elder care manager, start asking people in the area such as a faith community leader, the Alzheimer's Association (www. alz.org), your local Meals on Wheels agency (www.mowaa. org) or your local Area Agency on Aging (www.n4a.org), a federal agency in most counties. Ideally, an agency hires certified nursing assistants with some sort of RN/LVN or social worker oversight, which may cost more, but it is well worth it.

WORKING WITH AN AGENCY

Going with an agency has many advantages.

- Agencies should be licensed, insured, and bonded. For example, if a caregiver breaks or, on rare occasions, steals something, the agency will replace the item up to a certain value.

- An agency should do extensive background checks on all caregivers, including fingerprints.

- If a caregiver is ill or for some reason cannot fulfill the shift, the agency will send another caregiver usually within a certain time period.

- If you do not like a caregiver, the agency will send someone else.

- An agency provides worker's compensation if a caregiver is injured in your home.

- Some agencies have registered nurses and/or social workers who oversee the caregivers and make regular reports to family members. Sometimes there is an extra charge for this.

- ■ An agency will not allow caregivers to handle any money, checkbook, or bills. The agency will set up charge accounts at the grocery or pharmacy and will monitor the expenditure of money.

- ■ An agency can arrange for a professional bill payer to handle bills.

An agency caregiver costs $18.00 to $30.00 per hour at 2015 rates depending on geographical location. You can get caregivers for less on your own, but buyers beware! If you decide to find your own private caregiver, be sure to do the following:

- ■ Always ask for references.

- ■ Get recommendations from faith communities, local Area Agency on Aging, or local Alzheimer's Association.

- ■ Get arrangements in writing.

- ■ Ask them what they will do if they cannot fulfill a shift.

- ■ Pay for a background check, including fingerprints.

- ■ Determine who the private caregiver will take direction from.

- ■ Determine what happens if things in the home are missing.

- ■ Determine what happens if the private caregivers injure themselves on the job.

- ■ Determine what happens if there is gross negligence toward the patient.

- ■ Establish a sustained monitoring system and closely monitor the caregiver.

- ■ Never place a caregiver in charge of an elder's money, checkbook, or bill paying. Set up charge accounts at nearby grocery stores and pharmacies that the elder uses regularly and monitor those accounts.

At first, you may only need a few hours of care. Most agencies do not send anyone to a home for less than two hours. These two-hour visits can be arranged in the morning to get the elder out of bed, bathed, dressed, fed, medication reminders given, and settled for the day. If needed, they can come back in the evening to get the elder fed and ready for bed. Usually these two-hour visits cost $40.00 to $60.00 per visit at 2015 rates. As you can see, even brief visits can mount up. If you have one visit per day at $50.00, it is $350.00 per week or $1400.00 per month.

PAYING FOR IN-HOME CARE

Let's look at the cost for more extensive care in the home. Most people and almost all elders think that they will age in place, which means at home. And most elders think aging in place with a caregiver in the home is the least expensive way to age. They are shocked to find out that it is actually the most expensive care depending on the hours of care needed. Daily twenty-four-hour care in the home costs approximately $22,000 per month. Almost everyone asks if the government pays for any of this and is angered when they are told the government does not pay for this kind of care.

Long term care insurance does pay for this care if the elder bought the insurance and meets the criteria. Every long term care insurance policy is different, and depending on the type of policy you have purchased it may defray some of this cost. Sit down with your loved ones to discuss and become informed about the options and their costs. You can then make a reasonable plan knowing you have the resources to carry out that plan when the time comes or a crisis occurs.

When care in the home is difficult to afford, families may decide to pool their resources, money, and time to make up for the care needed.

In one case example, the family had five adult children in the area, and both parents needed twenty-four-hour care. After a rather contentious meeting with these adult children, some of whom wanted to participate and others who did not, we finally came up with a plan that worked. Using a calendar, we penciled in the times that each sibling was available. We then plugged those times into spaces where the agency caregiver was not present. They all agreed that each of them could stay one night a week which meant the agency caregiver would only be present two nights a week. Each adult child then gave an additional four hours during the daytime hours each week. One of the siblings could not give time, but offered to give money to help defray the cost of the agency caregiver. This cut the cost considerably and enabled this elderly couple to remain in their home. This scenario is not always possible but it is an option for some.

INFORMATION ABOUT PAID CAREGIVERS

Here are some tips about caregivers. These people do the most intimate and important care for our elderly for fairly low wages. Most of them are kind, conscientious, compassionate, and caring. It is not easy to go to someone's home you have never met and begin to give intimate personal care. When they come to your home, welcome them. Give them a chance for at least the first one or two shifts. If you have any concerns, discuss them with the agency and *not* with the caregiver.

When an elder is going to have agency caregivers, the following concerns usually come up.

◀ Just who are these people?

◀ Where do they come from?

◀ I do *not* want more than one caregiver. I just want one!

◀ I do not like strangers in my house!

◀ I do *not* want (name the race, gender, or the religion).

All of us, who do this work, know people do not want strangers coming into their home. It is natural to have some misgivings. That being said, you also have to be reasonable. Agencies have to abide by federal and state wage and hour laws. One caregiver cannot work 24/7 indefinitely, which is what some people demand.

This is how I answer these questions: "It is not easy to consider strangers coming to your home to assist you. These caregivers come from all corners of the world. Most of them, but not all, are women of color. They do speak, read, and understand English, but they may have an accent. I know you want consistency and the agency tries very hard to give you the same team of people as much as humanly possible, but people get sick, children get sick, cars break down, and then the agency will send a replacement. We, as an agency, must abide by the wage guidelines, which means that you will in all probability have more than one caregiver. If you have 24/7 care, you may have as many as five or six caregivers to cover the various shifts and time off each week. We are also an equal opportunity agency and cannot discriminate on the basis of race or religion."

If people are still resistant about having more than one caregiver, the explanation is as follows: "These folks are doing a job, and your home is their place of employment. They have families and lives of their own. They are like any other hard-working employee with designated hours and time off."

Some families or elders will then state they will find their own private caregiver, and they find one person who tells them they will do it all. This is simply not sustainable. They will eventually just not show up or will call in sick, or in some instances, send one of their family members to fulfill the shift. This scenario is a disaster waiting to happen.

In summary, anyone, regardless of the severity of their illness or decline, can be cared for at home. It depends on the financial resources to afford such care.

ALTERNATIVES TO CARE IN THE HOME

For many reasons, aging in place at home may not be the best scenario. People may be forced to age in a facility due to the lack of resources to age at home. On the other hand, some elders, at a certain age, freely make their own decision to select various facilities or retirement communities in which to age. They say it gives them peace of mind, freedom from care of home and property, and gives their adult children peace of mind. The decision may have nothing to do with financial resources. The following is a list of other options, the definitions of each option, and the approximate cost (knowing that costs will continue to rise and that costs vary in different parts of the country).

RETIREMENT COMMUNITIES

These are communities that offer homes, duplexes, or apartments for a monthly rent with no buy-in fee. You will get varying services such as meals, transportation to doctor appointments and shopping centers within a certain radius, activities, lectures, classes, entertainment, movies, laundry, and housekeeping. Depending on the facility, these offerings may vary. Retirement communities are for independent seniors who no longer want the responsibility of a large home and yard and are downsizing to a simpler lifestyle.

The cost varies depending on the luxury of the facility, housing type, whether you are single or a couple, and services. They may start as low as $1500.00 a month to $4,000.00 and up. Management may require a physical exam from a physician stating that the elder is independent and mentally able to manage his affairs without assistance.

Low cost housing for elders living on a tight budget is offered through Section 8 housing, a federal program, or other local non-profit programs. Rent may be as little as $700.00 per month with some amenities offered.

ASSISTED LIVING FACILITIES

These are either freestanding facilities or may be part of the above retirement communities available to an elder who is unable to perform ADLs or the IADLs without assistance. If already in a retirement complex, the elder may stay in their same living quarters and in other instances, she may have to move to a particular floor or area offering the needed assistance. Assisted living facilities generally do not include skilled nursing facility care. If that is needed, the elder needs to transfer out of the assisted living facility and into a SNF.

Assisted living facilities offer a variety of living options from a studio to two bedroom or more apartments, duplexes, or homes. Costs depend on whether you are single or a couple. They may charge an entrance fee of several thousand dollars depending on your choice and size of housing with some charging more for a view or upper floor. Monthly rent depending on your location, may start at $1500.00 for a studio and go up from there. Rents can rise yearly, ranging from two to four percent or more per year. When planning, ask the facility what the rent-increase history has been.

The cost may also vary depending on the amount of assistance needed. Assisted living facilities may charge a flat fee, or an *a la carte* basis. For instance, if an elder needs assistance with medication administration and dressing, the cost will be one amount. That amount increases each time an additional need is added. The cost varies, but is approximately $1500.00 to $5000.00 or higher per month, depending on location and assistance needed.

If you are looking for an assisted living facility in your area, the computer is a huge resource as are the National

Association of Area Agencies on Aging (www.n4a.org) Alzheimer's Association, (www.alz.org), American Association of Retired People (www.aarp.org), etc. These computer sites will give you criteria on how to judge a facility. You need to make an appointment and visit the facility. If choosing a facility is overwhelming or you are trying to do this as an adult child long distance, there are placement specialists in every city that will help you do this.

Remember, however, these specialists are often paid by the facilities for placing a client in that facility. There is no national organization for senior placement specialists and consequently no specific web site. You would need to enter *elder placement specialist* as your search criteria, and designate your geographic area. The National Geriatric Care Manager site, www.caremanager.org may also assist you in locating a placement specialist in your area.

When choosing any facility, find people who are using the facility, ask your physicians, your faith community leaders, and your local senior centers. Go visit the facility both scheduled and unscheduled. When visiting, ask the residents how they like living there. On a recent visit to an elder in an assisted living facility, I rode up in the elevator with several facility residents. I asked them all how they liked living there. A variety of responses were given, but they were all generally positive even when asked about the food!

ADULT FAMILY HOMES

These facilities are also known as board and care homes or residential care facilities. Each area of the country may use a different name. These are individual homes in a neighborhood that house approximately six elders needing some ADL assistance. Some take elders that have dementia symptoms. These homes are loosely monitored and regulated by the state in which they are located. They may or may not have a nurse owner or overseer. They are staffed with unskilled caregivers who may or may not be certified nursing assistants. The knowledge level and experience on the part of the owners and caregivers plus services offered vary widely, but all offer assistance with ADLs plus room and board. The cost is generally between $3,000.00 to $6,000.00 per month, and higher.

CONTINUING CARE RETIREMENT COMMUNITIES

Continuing Care Retirement Communities (CCRCs) are the Cadillac of elder living and care. You may enter as an independent elder and know that you will be taken care of no matter what may happen until your death. Many religious denominations have founded these communities and continue to support them in some way. They provide the gamut of care from independent living to assisted living to skilled nursing care including dementia care all on one campus or site.

These communities charge a substantial one time upfront fee from $100,000.00 up to a million dollars depending on your choice of housing and geographic location. You then pay a monthly fee from approximately $3,000.00 to $5,000.00 and up depending on your choice of home and care needed. The monthly fee will go up each year. Some may contract with a nearby skilled nursing facility off site. The contracts you sign when you join a CCRC vary widely, but most will give back a portion of the initial one-time fee if the elder dies within a

certain time period. Read the fine print on these contracts so you know what you are buying.

There are three main types of contracts for CCRCs.[2]

> *Life care (extended) contract.* Most expensive
> but gives the elder unlimited care services without
> additional charges.

> *Modified contract.* Offers specific services for a
> specific period of time. If the time expires, services
> will be available but at a higher cost per month.

> *Fee-for-service contract.* The entrance fee may be
> lower but any care needed will be paid at the market
> rate on an ongoing basis.

As in all the options, shop carefully. Visit these facilities
and ask people in the area what they know of these facilities. Ask your physician. Faith community leaders are
an excellent resource as they visit elders in these facilities
on a regular basis.

For those that can afford it, these communities offer
enormous peace of mind both for the elder and adult
children.

ADULT DAY CARE

For adults with dementia symptoms including Alzheimer's, or adults with chronic health conditions who need
companionship and supervision, adult day care is one
of the best cost effective options around. Adult day care
differs from senior centers, as day care elders need supervision and assistance with ADLs. This allows family
caregivers to have a break during the day and provides an
enriched environment for the elder. These are the biggest

bang for the buck so to speak, as many are non-profits, which provide a sliding scale fee depending on the ability to pay. Some even provide transportation to and from the elder's home. On average, the cost is approximately $60.00 per day with some centers as low as $35.00 per day and others as high as over $100.00 per day. Although Medicare does not pay for this care, Medicaid does pay, as do a few private insurances. Some centers offer scholarship help. These facilities are open Monday through Friday for eight to twelve hours depending on the facility.

There are three types of adult day care facilities.[3]

Social. Offers social activities, meals, and recreation in a safe, supervised environment.

Adult Day Health Care (ADHC). In addition to the social activities, offers health related services and usually has physical therapy, occupational therapy, speech therapy, a nurse on duty, possibly a social worker, care management, and a physician available. Some offer disease management services for chronic conditions as hypertension, diabetes, and cardiac conditions.

Adult day care for dementia disorders including Alzheimer's. Offers services and activities specifically geared for the elder with dementia symptoms.

These facilities are regulated to some degree, but each state has different standards, and some are very loosely regulated. The advantages of these facilities are caregiver relief and maintaining and supporting an elder by providing stimulating activities and nutrition. This support can often prevent future hospitalizations and can further rehab after hospitalizations and beyond. Using day care to maintain an elder's level of wellness can mean a delay in having to enter a long-term care facility.

You can find an adult day care program in your area by calling The Eldercare Locator at 1-800-677-1116 or www.eldercare.gov. The National Adult Day Services Association is also a good source for general information about services. Their number is 1-877-745-1440 or www.nadsa.org.

As with any care option, you have to decide what the elder and the caregiver need. Does the elder need simply a social model of day care, a health model, or a dementia model? What do you, as the caregiver need? Do you need transportation for the elder, and/or do you need extended hours due to your work schedule? All of these things determine which center you will use. Since these are so loosely regulated state by state, go and visit the centers near you. Talk with people who have used these centers. Talk with your faith community leaders, ask you physician, and ask your local senior center.

For some families, the term *adult daycare* has a negative connotation. Admitting an elder to care management and discussing with the family some options for their loved one with dementia, I suggested an adult daycare facility not far from their home. The response received was one of indignation and outrage. The devoted spouse said, "Do you know who this person is? He has been the CEO of an international company, founder of our local symphony, leader in his church for years, and an accomplished musician. You clearly do not know whom you are dealing with. Daycare! We will have none of it!"

After listening carefully to the litany of accomplishments, which were many and worthy, I said, "That was then and his accomplishments were truly remarkable; however, you called me because things have changed, and you are having difficulty managing the way things are now. We are talking about the now."

This is never an easy conversation to have with a client. The devoted spouse and caregiver may have called because she is at her wits end with a demented loved one, but is still clinging to the past trying to bring the past into the present. In this situation, I simply suggested that the spouse meet me at the daycare center and observe for a few hours. She reluctantly agreed, and eventually decided to accept this option.

Placement of a loved one in a facility/program of any kind is never easy and is often part of a long process. It means letting go of the past and giving up on a life and companionship one may have counted on for their elder years. This is a lonely road and one should not walk it alone. There are community resources like the Alzheimer's Association that can make this road not only easier but also far less lonely (www.alz.org). Care managers plus paid caregivers can also make this transition much easier.

MOVING IN WITH FAMILY MEMBERS

This option is fraught with minefields. This can be a successful venture or a real disaster. If you decide that you want to bring a frail elder (either physically frail or demented or both) into your home, there is one caveat to remember. *Do Not Think You Can Do This Alone.* This also applies to couples where one spouse is trying to take care of the other. **If you decide to make this commitment, schedule help right from the start. Do not wait until the devoted caregiver is so worn out and exhausted that it becomes a crisis.** I have seen over and over where a devoted caregiver becomes frail, ill, and actually dies from exhaustion trying to care for another frail elder. The same caveat applies to adult children who make this decision. Most people have no clue the time and energy needed to provide for a frail elder. It is a constant 24/7 proposition. I have seen some families that think their teenagers will help. Sometimes this works and other times, not so much.

One of the more tragic disasters I witnessed was a frail elder being cared for by his single adult son, who thought his teen-aged sons would help out. One day the boys were left in charge of the grandfather who was taking his daily nap. The boys decided to leave the house for a while with their friends. When they returned about an hour later, the elder had died trying to get out of bed. His head got caught between the bed rails and he accidently hung himself. This is an extreme example, but it demonstrates that if you do not go into this venture with your eyes wide open and get the help needed right from the beginning, bad things may happen.

Teenagers should not be in charge of an elder. They can certainly assist. This can be a loving, learning time, and a character-building period, but they should not be put in sole charge. You need to find help in other ways. I strongly recommend paid caregivers from an agency that allows you as a family to continue your lives and professions. If financially not feasible, then you need to look for options including placement or day care.

Many families are willing to help, but it is usually one family member physically closest to the elder who shoulders the responsibility. Other members may offer financial assistance and vague assurances they will help when they can. Everyone then goes back to their lives thinking all is well.

In one case, a long distance sister had arrived to relieve the sister who had the major responsibility of caring for their elder demented mother for the past three years. The newly arrived long distance sister had been the caregiver for three days. This is what she said:

"I have been here for three days and I am losing my mind! I do not know how my sister does this. She has been doing it without a break for three years, and I came here so she could have a three-week vacation. Can you help me?"

Help was soon on the way and a daily caregiver was at the house within the hour.

What really needed to occur, however, was a plan regarding what was going to happen when the sister returned from vacation. Over the next three weeks, the long distance sister and I sat down and began to draw up a plan for a much more equitable way to care for their mother. When the sister returned from her vacation and learned of the plan, she broke down and wept with relief. They did not believe they could financially continue as many hours with a paid caregiver, but they did keep some of the hours. One long distance sibling offered to pay for a housekeeper once every two weeks. Another sibling was enlisted to share some caregiving. The plan was defined, definite, and scheduled on the calendar. None of this, "I will help if and when I can."

We talked to their church leaders and found the church had a list of sitters who would provide a couple hours of sitting service several times a week for free. A neighbor who had been a long-time friend volunteered one afternoon a week to be with the elder. The caregiving sister had never reached out for help. When monies are tight, you may have to get creative, and everybody needs to shoulder some defined, definite, and scheduled responsibility.

There is a word of caution regarding volunteers. You need to be reasonable about volunteers if you are lucky enough to find them. These people are *not* there to provide personal care (transfers, bathing, toileting, dressing, cleaning, medication administration, etc.) They are there to sit with the elder and provide companionship plus safety monitoring in the case of a demented elder for a short time defined as a couple hours. They should have clear instructions regarding an emergency contact if things go wrong.

SKILLED NURSING FACILITIES

Skilled Nursing Facilities (SNF) are the dreaded nursing homes that give people nightmares. If you ask anyone what their greatest fears are about aging, you will hear the following, "I do not want to end up in a nursing home, and I do not want to lose my mind to Alzheimer's."

These facilities have changed drastically over the last twenty or more years. They are not the dreaded end-of-the-road places they used to be. In fact, it is quite hard to place an elder in a long-term SNF bed these days. The reason is this. What used to happen in hospitals now happens in nursing homes. If you have a knee or hip replacement, you will be discharged in a matter of two to three days. You either go home with support and help in the home or you will go to a SNF if you have no support. Hospitals will not discharge you to the home setting without some support. It used to be that you spent days in the hospital following joint replacement surgery and received your rehabilitation with physical therapy and occupational therapy in the hospital.

Again, using my own mother as an example, when she had her stroke in the mid-eighties, she spent over three weeks receiving physical and occupational therapy in the hospital! This is simply unheard of presently. You now will be sent to a SNF to receive rehabilitation therapy for joint replacements, stroke rehab, or cardiac rehab, and thus, many of us may see the inside of a SNF for a short period of time.

SNFs still provide the so-called long-term beds for the frail elderly, but they are hard to find as most beds have been turned over to the rehab business. I have tried at times to place an elder in a SNF when there have been no other options. On one case, I investigated four SNFs for a patient with MS, and there were waiting lists from six months to five years for a long-term bed. Furthermore, Medicare does not pay for long term custodial care in a SNF.

If you want Medicare to pay for a stay in a SNF, you have to qualify. You have to be a Medicare beneficiary, receive care from a Medicare certified SNF, and have a three-day qualifying stay in a hospital, (many hospital stays are less than three days.)

A doctor's order, and a skilled need (defined as a condition that requires the skills of a registered nurse or a physical therapist) must be documented. Medicare will pay *up to* one hundred days of skilled nursing care per illness. When working with families with loved ones in a nursing home, there is the mistaken belief that those hundred days are just a given. Comments like this are heard, "Oh we now have a hundred days to catch our breath and know Mom is taken care of." This is *not* the case. You only get to receive Medicare reimbursement if the skilled care shows improvement in the elder's condition. If there is a plateau in progress or a downturn, Medicare will no longer pay and other arrangements or options have to be considered.

"But Mom still needs care! How can they cut off Medicare payments?" This is where confusion reigns supreme. Remember the skilled need clause? The elder has to have a skilled need, which is something that requires the education and skill level of a registered nurse or a physical therapist or in some cases a speech therapist. "Custodial care which is non-skilled care like incontinence care (adult brief changes), bathing, dressing, eating, toileting, does not require a college educated professional. Although the elder may need some care, meaning custodial care, Medicare does not pay for that. Medicare only pays for skilled care and *only* if the care assists elders to recover from their condition.

About fifty percent of all nursing home residents must pay for their own care out of their personal finances. The average annual cost is approximately $60,000 per year and rising, with costs varying by state and care needed. If financial resources are depleted, an elder may become eligible for Medicaid, which is a state and federal program that may pay for SNF care if you are eligible. Check with your state for eligibility requirements. In the present day, SNFs are a last resort for most people. If all this seems complicated, it's because it *is* complicated

If placement in any facility or care community including a SNF is going to be the option chosen, experience has showed me that placement nearest a concerned adult child is wise. Even though there may be a posh, beautiful facility fifty miles away versus one that is closer to the adult child with a good quality of care but not so posh, choose the closer facility. First, you will visit your elder parent more often if it does not require a long drive and time commitment. Second, the squeaky wheel gets the oil. If you are visiting the facility often and staff knows you and what you expect, your loved one is going to get more attention. Facility staff may disagree with this, but I have seen it repeatedly. Choose a suitable facility nearby, so frequent visits are possible.

In the past decade, there has been a movement in this country regarding SNFs, and it is called the Eden movement. The following summary gives some trends happening all over the country in terms of SNFs.[4]

> Nursing home care has long been focused on the medical care of patients. However, new trends in nursing point to a fuller experience for both the senior and the caregivers. Here are a few visionary places that are sparking a culture change in long-term care:
>
> *The Pioneer Network.* Formed in 1997, the Pioneer Network is dedicated to the idea that long-term care should be an opportunity to thrive, not simply decline. This culture-change movement is

transforming provider-centered nursing care to a consumer-centered experience, thus offering more control, independence, and dignity to seniors who require long-term care. A large part of the Pioneer Network's plan of action is transforming institutional nursing homes into comfortable, real home settings.

The Eden Alternative. The core concept of the Eden Alternative is simple: rather than see long-term care facilities as places for the old and frail, they should be seen as places where the elderly can thrive and age gracefully. Rather than sterile nursing homes, the Eden Alternative sees communities, neighborhoods, and homes as the best way to promote a healthy atmosphere while providing the physical, medical, and emotional support every individual requires.

The Green House Project. Inspired by the Eden Alternative, the Green House Project relies on a triple concept: Warm, Smart, and Green. The facilities are warmly decorated and have a sense of community, but they are also built smart, with wireless paging systems, electronic lifting devices, and the like. Just as the name implies, the Green House Project stays green by making good use of sunlight, plants, and outdoor spaces for seniors to enjoy.

"Seniors in nursing homes are not waiting to die. They just need a bit of help to live a purposeful, happy life. The culture change of nursing care reflects this shift in thinking, not only in the places offered for senior living, but in the very core of the nursing care system. Even the vocabulary is changing by focusing on the senior as a whole and vital person, rather than a number on a chart.

As the culture change in long-term care slowly takes hold, the lives of seniors are changing for the better. These are not the nursing homes your grandmother knew, and as the trend continues, more seniors may experience the philosophy of the Pioneer Network, the Eden Alternative, and the Green House Project as the rule, rather than the exception."[5]

COMMUNAL AGING FACILITIES

for elders without family

Another alternative to aging facilities is the communal aging facility or organization. These are communities of elders who have gathered together to either live in a small enclave, which they have financed, or elders who live in an area and are organized to give help to one another as the need arises. Although these are fairly new concepts and can look very different from one another, they seem to be an increasing option.

In the February 27, 2006 *New York Times*, there was an article on Glacier Circle, an elder commune, one of the country's first self-planned housing developments for the elderly. These elders organized, bought land, hired an architect, and built their own community. According to this article, there are now eighty-two such communities across the country.

HOW DO WE PAY FOR LONG-TERM CARE?

So how do we pay for long-term care either at home or at a facility? There are not a lot of options.

◖ Private pay, which means the money comes from the family resources.

◖ Long term care insurance. This is insurance, which the elder has bought and paid for each month over a period of time and for which the elder must qualify before the insurance pays a benefit.

◖ Medicaid in some states and some circumstances.

◖ Reverse Mortgage.

When called to meet with an elder and/or their family, the discussion quickly turns to, "how much is this going to cost?" I have gotten over my surprise by some of the answers when families discover the cost. The following are some replies when discussing finances:

"Well how do you expect me to pay for that? I am not made of money. Doesn't the government pay for this?"

"I have the money but I do not want to waste it on THAT!"

"I do not want to spend money on care. I have saved all my life so I can leave something for Junior."

"I do not know why we have to spend this kind of money on the old man. He is just going to die anyway."

"I was counting on Dad's money to send my son to college. At the rate we are going, the money will be gone."

Sometimes answers go like this:

> "Do whatever it takes to care for Mom. Money is no object."
>
> Or, "Spare no expense. I want her to have the highest standard of care."
>
> Or, "We need to watch our resources, so we would like a combination of agency care and will augment with family caregivers."

I make no judgments regarding these responses. Feelings and emotions are neither right or wrong, good or bad. It is what we do with these feelings that count. The job as care manager is to try to help elders and their families find the resources to provide the care needed. People naturally want to protect their assets and are often very secretive about these assets. Money is a private and very emotional issue.

After listening carefully to an elder's objections, I try to explain that this is an important use of their resources. Saving for an adult child and denying yourself or your spouse the care needed is a poor use of money. Adult children, who may have been counting on the estate for their own future, need to realize that the estate is not theirs until their parents have died.

It is not unusual for an elder to deny having the funds needed for care, but when asked if they own their own house, they will say something like this, "I not only own my house but it is paid for!" They are proud of this and rightfully so. The house is a valuable asset and can provide a resource for needed care. It is called a reverse mortgage. As a care manager, I helped several elders get a reverse mortgage, and remain in their homes with the needed care. Some people including some elder law attorneys, however, are very opposed to this route for various reasons, mainly the cost of obtaining a reverse mortgage. A reverse mortgage means you can borrow against the equity of your home. You and your spouse must be sixty-two years or older. In a reverse mortgage, the lender pays you a lump sum or monthly payments based on the equity of your home. You owe nothing until you die or move. You or your estate then pays back the loan amount plus interest. It may mean that there is less or nothing for heirs. Before getting a reverse mortgage, be sure that you can afford the ongoing maintenance and property taxes that owning any home incurs. This is a big decision and one that should be made only after getting professional financial advice and discussing it with family members.

In summary, there is no elder that cannot receive care at home no matter how ill or disabled they are, if the financial resources are available. To receive care at home may be financially feasible if the hours required are small; however, as the needs increase due to changing conditions, so will the number of care hours and the cost.

FINANCIAL EXAMPLES: IN-HOME AND OUT-OF-HOME

Here are some examples of costs for various services from the 2014 Genworth survey.[6]

USA, 2014

		Minimum	Median	Maximum	Median Annual Rate	Five-year Annual Growth
Home	Homemaker Services hourly rates	$8	$19	$39	$43,472	1%
Home	Home Health Aid Services hourly rates	$9	$20	$39	$45,188	1%
Community	Adult Day Health Care daily rates	$12	$65	$215	$16,900	3%
Facility	Assisted Living Facility (one bedroom single occupancy) monthly rates	$750	$3,500	$10,412	$42,000	4%
Facility	Nursing Home (semi-private room) daily rates	$94	$212	$800	$77,380	4%
Facility	Nursing Home (private room) daily rates	$104	$240	$954	$87,600	4%

Here are three samples from the 2014 Genworth survey illustrating the differences on the West coast, Midwest, and East coast.

WASHINGTON STATE, 2014

		Minimum	Median	Maximum	Median Annual Rate	Five-year Annual Growth
Home	Homemaker Services hourly rates	$16	$23	$30	$51,777	3%
Home	Home Health Aid Services hourly rates	$16	$23	$30	$52,624	3%
Community	Adult Day Health Care daily rates	$17	$67	$144	$17,443	3%
Facility	Assisted Living Facility (one bedroom single occupancy) monthly rates	$1,000	$4,250	$9,000	$51,000	6%
Facility	Nursing Home (semi-private room) daily rates	$100	$253	$362	$92,345	4%
Facility	Nursing Home (private room) daily rates	$190	$280	$434	$102,018	4%

Rate Range

IOWA, 2014

| | | Rate Range | | | Median Annual Rate | Five-year Annual Growth |
		Minimum	Median	Maximum		
Home	Homemaker Services hourly rates	$16	$22	$35	$49,764	2%
Home	Home Health Aid Services hourly rates	$16	$22	$35	$50,771	2%
Community	Adult Day Health Care daily rates	$18	$55	$150	$14,300	3%
Facility	Assisted Living Facility (one bedroom single occupancy) monthly rates	$930	$3,418	$8,620	$41,016	4%
Facility	Nursing Home (semi-private room) daily rates	$120	$169	$259	$61,685	4%
Facility	Nursing Home (private room) daily rates	$135	$185	$289	$67,525	4%

CONNECTICUT, 2014

| | | ── Rate Range ── | | | | |
		Minimum	Median	Maximum	Median Annual Rate	Five-year Annual Growth
Home	Homemaker Services hourly rates	$13	$20	$25	$44,616	1%
Home	Home Health Aid Services hourly rates	$15	$22	$31	$49,192	0%
Community	Adult Day Health Care daily rates	$70	$80	$144	$20,800	2%
Facility	Assisted Living Facility (one bedroom single occupancy) monthly rates	$2,000	$5,289	$9,200	$63,468	7%
Facility	Nursing Home (semi-private room) daily rates	$266	$390	$550	$142,168	3%
Facility	Nursing Home (private room) daily rates	$296	$425	$595	$155,125	3%

TASK LIST

☐ PLAN FOR YOUR AGING JOURNEY BY DISCUSSING YOUR FINANCIAL RESOURCES WITH FAMILY AND/OR ELDER LAW ATTORNEY.

☐ DECIDE ON SEVERAL OPTIONS THAT YOU CAN AFFORD.

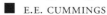

CHAPTER SIX
SOCIALIZATION

In this Chapter...

WORKING WITH SOCIAL SUPPORT SYSTEMS

When an elder care manager does an assessment, one of the most important aspects of that assessment is socialization and support in the elder's life. More often than not, at that point in time, the support and socialization systems have declined to very little or nil. Friends may have moved away or died, a lifetime partner may have died, adult children may live far away, or neighbors may no longer find it productive to maintain the friendship. Driving may no longer be an option. The elder's world has shrunk. People do not survive well in this circumstance either physically or mentally.

Fortunately, many communities have risen to the challenge and created resources for the elders in their community. The following are some resources that elder care managers use regularly. It may mean that family members, if they live nearby, need to provide transportation or a caregiver may need to be hired to provide transportation plus some supervision.

SENIOR CENTERS

Alive and busy places, they have nominal fees and are fully utilized until their seams are bursting. I am using one right now in my community as I take art classes at the center. Sometimes I cannot find a place to park because there is such a variety of services and programs being offered. For example, a variety of arts and crafts are being taught, one room was full with men and women playing mahjong. Another room was full with people playing cards. The computer room was full with a waiting line, a delicious hot lunch was being served in the dining room, a grief counseling session was being held in one room, tax help was being offered in another. A current event lecture was going on in another room. If there is one of these nearby, take advantage of all they have to offer even if the elder has some dementia.

According to the National Council on Aging (NCOA), "senior centers have become one of the most widely used services among America's older adults. Today, 11,400 senior centers serve more than one million older adults every day."[1]

The NCOA goes on to state, "senior centers serve as a gateway to the nation's aging network — connecting older adults to vital community services that can help them stay healthy and independent."[2]

Their funding comes from a variety of sources, including federal and state options. They also rely heavily on volunteer hours. The cost to the elder is nominal. Some charge a yearly membership fee of $10.00 while others may not. Meals are approximately $6.00 a meal. They offer a wealth of opportunities as follows:

◄ Meals and nutrition programs

◄ Information and assistance

◄ Health, fitness, and wellness programs

◄ Transportation services

◄ Public benefits counseling

◄ Employment assistance

◄ Volunteer and civic engagement opportunities

◄ Social and recreational activities

◄ Educational and arts programs

◄ Intergenerational programs [3]

"Research shows that older adults who participate in senior center programs can learn to manage and delay the onset of chronic disease and experience measurable improvements in their physical, social, spiritual, emotional, mental, and economic well-being."[4]

Caregiver care plans should include transportation of elders to these centers, and instructions for the caregiver to stay with the elder to help the elder negotiate socialization skills with others. It may take a savvy caregiver to have these skills, but it can be done.

ADULT DAY CARE CENTERS

We have already discussed these in a previous chapter (see "Adult Day Care" on page 99), but these programs provide wonderful socialization opportunities especially for elders with dementia symptoms.

FAITH COMMUNITIES

Faith communities provide community building and socialization for the elderly, and they cost nothing or very little. Faith communities host book groups, Bible study, movie nights, lecture series, grief support groups, and more. They often provide meals for people who are living alone especially around major holidays. These communities often offer support groups for people who have suffered major losses and are dealing with grief. If an elder has a faith community, it is important for a care manager or family member to contact the faith leader and let them know that additional support is needed. Many faith communities have a member of their leadership staff or volunteers who visit the sick and elderly on a regular basis. They may also provide transportation to activities and services. These visits can be the highlight of the week for some elders.

FRIENDLY VISITORS PROGRAMS

Your local Alzheimer's Association often has a friendly visitor program. These are volunteers who will visit an elder in the home or facility on a regular basis.

FRIENDS AND NEIGHBORS

It is sometimes possible to arrange for friends and neighbors to visit regularly on a rotating basis. This may take a bit of organizing, but it is sometimes a great success. These visits do not have to be long or involved. Sometimes a regular mealtime visit can be arranged.

ELDERS WHO VOLUNTEER

Elders form a vital service as volunteers in their community thus improving socialization opportunities by giving valuable time and skill where needed. Food banks, animal welfare centers, churches, libraries, schools, are all places that use elder volunteers.

Placement facilities such as retirement communities, assisted living, adult family homes, even skilled nursing facilities use elder volunteers.

All these facilities offer an enormous variety of opportunities for socialization and activity. If the resources are available, there is no one that cannot be cared for at home if that is the goal. That being said, sometimes home is not necessarily the best place to be. Home can be very isolating for an elder, and I have seen some elders come back to life when placed in the appropriate community or facility. It all comes down to goals and resources for the *Journey through Old*. For this reason, it is vital for the elder to sit down with his/her support group/family and plan ahead.

Elder care managers and/or family members can build socialization into every care plan and make arrangements for these activities to take place regularly during the week depending on the elder's energy and endurance level. Socialization needs to be defined, definite, scheduled, and monitored. *Be Creative*.

Now that we have all the pieces in place, let's look at how this might play out with an actual elder.

CASE STUDY: THE ISSUES WITH ISOLATION

 Mary was eighty-six years old living by herself since her husband died five years ago. She had three children who lived in various parts of the country far from Mary. One of the children was estranged from her mother, but the other two were somewhat attentive and visited once a year. Mary's financial situation had deteriorated since her husband's death, plus she had a decline in funds due to the economic recession. She basically lived on her social security, a small pension, and an annuity set up by her spouse before he died. She had owned and lived in the same house for the past forty years and no longer had a mortgage. She lived on approximately $40,000.00 per year.

Mary's home had not been updated since she and her husband had bought the house with the exception of a fairly new roof and some new plumbing. Mary was still driving, although recently had two fender benders and was no longer driving at night. She fell at home in the bathroom shortly before Thanksgiving, prompting one of her daughters to arrange a visit for the holiday.

Although not badly injured in the fall, she had hit her head and needed stitches at the emergency room. An attentive neighbor had heard her call for help through an open window or she might have lain on the floor for an indefinite period of time. Mary was still grieving over the loss of her spouse of fifty years but was adamant about remaining independent in her own home. Like many widows, she had become somewhat socially isolated due to her grief and reluctance to go out without a spouse.

Her daughter, June, decided to come for Thanksgiving, given the recent events. When June arrived, she was stunned at her mother's condition. Her mother had lost about fifteen pounds, and seemed confused. The house was in a state of disorder, which was unlike her mother's past fastidiousness. June immediately started to clean and cook for her mother, but she was extremely concerned about the future especially when she needed to get back to her own family in a week.

She noticed during her stay that her mother was no longer taking her prescribed medications because she could not remember what she was supposed to take and when to take them. June called her siblings and expressed her concern about the future and her feeling she could not leave her mother in her present condition. Neither of her other siblings were able to offer any solutions, so June, in desperation, called an agency offering care management and caregivers to assist her mother after she left.

An agency RN care manager made an appointment to come to the home to listen to June and her mother. This visit included a full assessment of medical needs, especially medication regimes, paperwork (a will or trust, durable power of attorney for health and finance, personal health record), safety issues especially in light of the recent falls, and quality of life issues since Mary was increasingly isolated due to the loss of her spouse.

After listening and assessing, the RN care manager then drew up a plan of care, which she shared with Mary and June.

The plan of care addressed all the issues found from listening to Mary and June, and the assessment findings. Since Mary was adamant about staying in her home, the plan of care included the following:

Safety issues. In light of recent falls and driving fender benders, Mary was placed on a fall prevention program, and several home safety issues were addressed. These included the following:

◀ Install grab bars in the shower and by the toilet.

◀ Remove throw rugs to reduce tripping hazards.

◀ Increase lighting throughout the house.

◀ Install railings on all stairs.

◀ Cease all driving with a plan for future transportation needs.

It was clear that Mary was having a decline in her ability to perform IADLs such as housework, transportation, bill paying, laundry, and securing groceries. She still was able to perform her ADLs (transferring, walking, toileting herself, bathing, dressing, and eating).

Medical issues.

◀ Since Mary was not taking her medications as directed, the care manager contacted Mary's physician to clarify what Mary should be taking.

◀ Since the physician had not seen Mary in well over a year, an appointment was made for the near future. Once the medication regime was confirmed, recommendations were made to assure Mary was complying with these orders.

◖ Since it had been a couple of years with no dental or foot care, appointments were made with these practitioners.

◖ As no family members lived close by, recommendations were made to have an RN come every two weeks to fill Mary's mediplanners, assess compliance, and to explore the possibilities of a local advocate to assist with Mary's medication compliance, keeping in mind that financial resources were limited.

◖ Due to weight loss, it was discovered on the assessment that Mary was eating sporadically and was becoming malnourished and dehydrated (eating mostly tea and toast). It was recommended that a trained agency caregiver come daily for four hours to assist Mary with her IADLs, assess safety issues on an ongoing basis, provide transportation including grocery shopping and rides to appointments, provide daily fall prevention measures such as stand by assist, do laundry, light housekeeping, provide companionship especially at meal times, assure medication compliance, and prepare healthy meals and hydration to Mary's liking.

◖ Addressing Mary's confusion, a recommendation was made to refer her to her primary physician with the possibility of a neurologist consult. June was tasked with finding documents such as the location of her mother's will and need for updating, if necessary. Also, she needed to discuss with her mother and implement a durable power of attorney for health care and finance plus initiate a personal health record as well as help her mother find a local advocate.

Social issues. Due to Mary's isolation, socialization and quality of life issues were addressed.

The care manager did a depression assessment, which showed signs of depression. The primary care physician was notified of this finding so it could be addressed at the upcoming visit which either the care manager or local advocate would also attend.

It was recommended that Mary participate in a senior center quite near her home. Mary would receive a hot lunch twice a week and would be meeting and talking with other seniors. The center also provided a grief support group for seniors who had lost their spouses. The agency caregiver would be providing transportation to these events.

It was also recommended that the care manager continue to see Mary once or twice a month to assess progress or lack thereof, oversee the caregiver, and make any adjustments to the care plan. The care manager would stay in touch with a designated family member who would then disseminate the information to the rest of the family.

When the assessments were completed and recommendations were presented including the monthly costs, both Mary and June were aghast at the proposed cost. A financial assessment was completed, and a search began to examine where the monies might come from. The care manager organized a family meeting via a conference call at the agency office where all the adult children were invited to participate, even the estranged daughter.

The care manager had prepared all the options including possible placement in an assisted living facility. At Mary's present level of care, most of the options were about the same financially. In the future, if Mary experienced a sudden or gradual decline, other options might prove more financially feasible than care in the home. At present, everyone was attempting to honor Mary's fervent wish to remain at home.

The conference lasted about ninety minutes with the bulk of the discussion around how to finance the care. All three children decided to contribute varying amounts and made a commitment to keep their mother at home as long as possible. Finally, the financial piece fell into place with a small amount coming from Mary's resources and the rest coming from the adult children. The care manager gave positive feedback to the adult children for making this possible while at the same time cautioned that Mary's care needs would probably increase in the not too distant future thus increasing the cost.

The necessary paper work was signed. This included the family members signing their agreement to the care plan. The care was initiated the following day.

CASE STUDY: FINANCIAL CARE PLAN

Here is a cost example of Mary's complete care plan, remembering that costs do vary determined by geographic area. These costs will rise each year.

- ■ Handy person to install two grab bars and two stair railings at $60.00 per hour for six hours= $360.00 one-time expense.

- ■ Set aside $50.00 per month for taxi service ongoing.

- ■ Agency caregiver hired for IADLs for four hours a day, seven days a week at $25.00 per hour = $3,000.00 per month.

- ■ Dental cleaning and other dental services (if no dental insurance) $200.00 every six months.

- ■ RN oversight every two weeks at $100.00 per visit = $200.00 per month (some agencies offer this at no cost if a caregiver is hired).

- ■ Updating documents with an elder law attorney $500.00 one-time expense.

- ■ Senior Center expense $10.00 membership per year, meals three times a week at $6.00 per meal = $72.00 per month.

Costs will be organized into one-time costs and ongoing costs.

ONE-TIME COSTS

One-time costs include the installation of safety equipment, elder attorney costs, and senior center membership.

Safety equipment installation	$360.00
Elder attorney	$500.00
Senior Center membership	$10.00
Total (one-time costs)	$870.00

ONGOING EXPENSES

Ongoing expenses include dental, hired caregiver, RN oversight, taxi, and senior center meals.

Taxi service	$50.00/month
Dental care	$200.00/every 6 months
Agency caregiver	$3000/month
RN oversight	$200.00/month
Senior center meals (12 total)	$72.00/month
Total	$3522

Total of both categories	***$4392***

If you figure in the monthly dental expense at approximately $33.00 per month the monthly expense for this care plan minus the one-time costs is ***$3355.00 or $40,260.00 per year***. This represents just the care plan expenses, and Mary will have other expenses as well. If the family cannot make up the rest of the monies Mary needs, the plan could be adjusted.

The caregiver could come every other day if Mary's condition permits. The RN oversight could be reduced to once a month, with a volunteer to fill the mediplanner or have the medications bubble packed so medications would only need to be filled once a month. Senior center meals could be reduced to once or twice a week. The fact remains, however, that Mary will decline in the future, and her needs will increase over time.

TASK LIST

☐ PLAN FOR AND MAKE SOCIALIZATION PART OF YOUR DAILY LIFE.

☐ KNOW THE COMMUNITY RESOURCES THAT WILL FACILITATE SOCIALIZATION AND A SENSE OF COMMUNITY BEFORE A CRISIS EVOLVES.

☐ CONSIDER VOLUNTEERING.

*"Life is ours to be spent,
not to be saved."*
■ D.H. Lawrence

CHAPTER SEVEN

NUTRITION & ELDERS (BEYOND TEA & TOAST)

In this Chapter…

■ MANAGING NUTRITION

■ REASONS FOR APPETITE LOSS AND POOR NUTRITION

■ ESTABLISHING A NUTRITIOUS MEAL PLAN

MANAGING NUTRITION

Good nutrition affects all aspects of our physical health and wellbeing, but it is so much more. Eating is a social experience. Since time began, people sat around the campfire and ate a community meal. If the food is not only nutritious but also sublimely delicious, and when it is coupled with great conversation with loving family or friends, the meal can almost be a religious experience!

Compare that picture with the way many elders live today. They are often marginalized in their individual homes or apartments either as couples or as widowed or divorced singles. For many of them, Meals on Wheels (MOWs) may be their only source of nutrition, which they eat alone. I am not disparaging Meals on Wheels. They are a wonderful program at a reasonable cost, and many elders would be unable to survive without them. MOW is funded by a combination of federal monies and local resources. Their goal is to combat and solve the hunger of nearly nine million seniors in America. The fee for each meal is between $3.00 and $4.00. If elders are unable to pay, they receive the meals anyway.[1] However, some elders just pack the trays in the freezer or refrigerator and do not eat them. I have, on numerous occasions, opened an elder's refrigerator or freezer and seen every shelf packed with MOWs uneaten. When I ask them why they are not eating the meals, they just vaguely answer something like, "Oh I am just tired of them." Or, "I just do not feel like eating them anymore." In the meantime, they may be losing weight and may actually be clinically malnourished and dehydrated. If your loved one is receiving MOWs, monitor to be sure the meals are being eaten.

WHAT IS NUTRITION AND
WHY IS IT SO IMPORTANT?

The science of nutrition helps us understand how the nutrients in food are processed by our bodies to promote good health. One day, my little five-year-old granddaughter and I were talking about gas for the car and how nice it would be if we could just pour anything into our cars and they would go. She suggested some soda pop and doughnuts and then she got more creative. "What if we could just pee into the gas tank and the car would go." As we both got even more creative, she was laughing and gasping between words saying, "Oh Grandma, you are so silly!"

Am I? Silly? We put the most outrageous things into our bodies — voluminous amounts of sugar, all kinds of unhealthy fats, gallons of soda, processed foods, alcohol, etc. We do not exercise. As a culture we are obese and sedentary, leading to all kinds of chronic illnesses as we age, such as type 2 diabetes, heart disease, respiratory illnesses due to smoking, abuse of both illegal drugs and prescription medications. It is not unlike putting junk in our gas tanks, and then we expect that our bodies will operate seamlessly for the better part of a hundred years!

We cannot prevent aging. What we can do is exercise daily and eat the types of food that fuel our bodies, maintaining them in an optimum condition for as long as possible throughout our life. It may not always work, but it is really the only option we have to age gracefully on this *Journey through Old*, and hopefully prevent some of the chronic illnesses that plague too many elders.

REASONS FOR APPETITE LOSS
AND POOR NUTRITION

There are many reasons elders may lose interest in eating with accompanying weight loss and nutritional deficits. Eating alone is often cited. "Without Joe, I just do not feel like fixing a meal for myself." In these instances, where a beloved spouse has died, the remaining elder may resort to eating small meals during the day consisting of tea and toast or something similar, whenever he feels hungry. Obviously this quickly leads to nutritional deficiencies and weight loss.

Some other reasons are as follows:

◀ Painful or ill-fitting dentures

◀ Loss of most or all teeth

◀ Not wanting to eat alone

◀ Depression

◀ Difficulty in obtaining groceries

◀ Lack of financial resources to buy groceries

◀ Decline in ability to smell or taste food

◀ Visual deficits making preparation of food difficult

◀ Decrease of appetite due to lack of exercise

◀ Chronic illnesses and medications that decrease appetite

◀ Alcoholism

◀ Dementia

Often these reasons are not discovered or addressed for a long time and result in serious weight loss, dehydration, and nutritional imbalances including electrolyte imbalances, trace mineral imbalances, vitamin deficiencies, etc. These imbalances and weight loss can result in serious behavior issues and significant changes in an elder's condition. As a care manager, it is one of the first things to assess. As a family member, if you notice any weight loss and changes in behavior, assess for causes by looking at the following signs and symptoms.

SIGNS OF NUTRITIONAL DEFICIENCIES

■ Unintentional or involuntary significant weight loss defined as:

When involuntary weight loss exceeds ten percent of usual weight (in nonobese persons), the source and potential result of weight loss must be investigated. Involuntary weight loss exceeding twenty percent of usual weight is often associated with severe protein-energy malnutrition, nutritional deficiencies, and multiorgan dysfunction.[2]

■ Significant losses of spouse, friend, pet, or vision.

■ Lack of food or large amounts of spoiled food in refrigerator or freezer.

■ Changes in behaviors and/or physical condition.

■ Grief and/or depression.

■ Signs of dehydration such as dry mouth, dry lips, poor skin elasticity.

■ Constipation or diarrhea.

 ■ Social isolation.

■ When visiting an elder at meal times, noticing that very little is being prepared or eaten.

■ When elder is asked what they are eating for breakfast, lunch, or dinner, getting a vague, inadequate answer.

IF AN ELDER'S NUTRITION DECLINES

Take action. Have the elder assessed by his/her primary care physician who will order blood tests to determine any deficiencies that need to be addressed. The physician, elder, and family will try to determine the cause of loss of appetite and poor nutritional intake. If these are readily obvious, plans need to be made and implemented. Often, however, things are not that black and white. This is what happened to my own mother when she lost her spouse after sixty years of marriage.

STORY: MY OWN MOTHER

 As stated earlier, my mother's grief over the loss of her husband caused a significant thirty-pound weight loss and a dramatic change in behavior. Her physician hospitalized her immediately due to low potassium and an electrolyte imbalance. Her grief and resulting depression also needed to be addressed.

Her nutritional deficiencies were quickly remedied and stabilized, but her depression was far more problematic resulting in the necessity of moving her near my brother and me where she could have close monitoring and socialization. Her grief and depression coupled with her isolation during meal times simply overwhelmed her. She had no desire to prepare food or eat by herself. She had rapidly slipped into the "tea and toast" routine on a daily basis.

ESTABLISHING A NUTRITIOUS MEAL PLAN

As an elder care manager, one of the first things to do for elders is to make sure they have well prepared nutritious meals. In more serious cases, a nutritionist may be needed to assess the elder and draw up specific meal plans. If a caregiver is going to be hired, the care manager may work with the caregiver in preparing delicious meals. It is wonderful if a caregiver comes to an agency and is already an accomplished cook!

In one community where I worked, there was a company that delivered meals on a regular basis from the elder's favorite restaurant. Some grocery stores like Safeway will deliver groceries or items from their deli. Amazon will deliver groceries in some cities, but this requires a computer to order the groceries. Another company called Magic Kitchen will ship prepared meals to your door arriving two or three days after you order. You can order online or call them toll free at 1-877-516-2442. The current cost of a two-serving entrée is between $10.00 to $35.00 depending on how labor intensive it is and the type of entrée. If you chose to order an entrée for two for $18.00, the shipping is $24.00 making the total $42.00. Clearly this might work for some but not others due to the cost.

In most communities, there are people who are personal chefs. These entrepreneurs are individuals usually with some chef background and credentials who have started their own business preparing meals for people in the customer's home using your own kitchen and equipment. Others may prepare meals in their own health department approved commercial kitchens and will deliver the foods to you. You can find a personal chef online by entering personal chef and your zip code.[3]

As a care manager, I have used these people on a number of occasions with very good results. Again there is a cost and a delivery charge. An example in the Seattle area at current rates for a couple (six meals for two people) is approximately $230 for both the food and the service costs, which comes to a little less than $20.00 per person per meal.

Do not overlook Meals on Wheels in the elder's community. As stated before, they are the most reasonable option for healthy balanced meals.

In some communities, there may be volunteers who bring food to the elderly either through faith communities or individuals who are simply good neighbors. This is usually not sustainable, however, for an extended need.

Seeing an elder go from losing weight with no interest in food to consuming healthy homemade meals daily and thriving is one of the greatest satisfactions. Caregivers can be coached and educated not only to prepare meals but also eat with the elder providing some companionship around eating. Caregivers may need to be taken to the store and shown what to buy and how to prepare food.

Recently, I took a caregiver to a local grocery store, showed her nutrient-rich foods to buy, and then showed her how to prepare them. The next time I went to the elder's home, the apartment was filled with the good smell of fresh food being prepared and cooked. This particular elder gained about fifteen pounds in a matter of a few weeks going from 98 pounds to 115 pounds. The caregiver was a good match in terms of companionship, which slowly helped to lift the elder's depression.

Eventually this elder was strong enough that the caregiver and elder would sometimes go out for dinner! This kind of care can make a world of difference in an elder's life. In this particular case, there was not a great pile of resources so the caregiver did two visits a day —in the morning she prepared a healthy breakfast, made a lunch for the elder to eat midday, and then came back in the evening to prepare dinner and eat with the elder. On these visits, she gave medication reminders and watched to make sure the medications were taken. Even small amounts of care and support can make a huge difference.

RESOURCES FOR NUTRITIONAL INFORMATION

This is not a book on nutritional regimes. There are many fine books on this topic, so I will be brief. Some may think they cannot afford fresh, whole foods that are well prepared. Think again! Malnutrition and dehydration are far more expensive to treat. What is meant by fresh, whole foods? Whole foods are those that are close to the earth. In other words, they have not been changed or processed but appear in the store or market just like they came out of the ground or off the tree.

Michael Pollan, in his groundbreaking book, *Omnivores Dilemma: A Natural History of Four Meals*, describes in a very succinct way how we all should be eating. It goes like this. Eat whole foods in season. Something your Grandmother would recognize. (She would not recognize Cheetos!) Eat mostly fruits and vegetables (with the emphasis on the vegetables) and not too much. Avoid fast food and processed food.[4]

An elder care manager will often bring in a nutritionist or dietitian to consult with the elder in terms of likes and dislikes. They can also assist in instructing the caregiver. As we age, the amount of food, the times we eat, and the consistency of food may change. Elders may find "three squares" a day too much, and they may prefer five small meals throughout the day, or they may prefer to eat much later or earlier than in the past.

Resources for elder nutrition are on the Internet. Here are two that are easy to use and helpful.

■ www.healthlinkbc.ca/pdf/HEFS_english.pdf

■ www.helpguide.org/life/senior_nutrition.htm

Two cookbooks available on Amazon.com are as follow:

■ *The Healthy Seniors Cookbook* by Marilyn McFarlane

■ *Diabetic Cooking for Seniors* by Kathleen Stanley

WORKING AROUND PHYSICAL EATING ISSUES

Some elders lose the ability to swallow their food and fluids with or without coughing and choking. This aspiration condition needs to be evaluated by a physician and a speech therapist. If the elder is diagnosed as an aspirator, meaning some food and fluids are going into the lungs, the physician and speech therapist will make some recommendations which may include thickening fluids (thin fluids are the hardest to swallow) and pureeing foods. It is important to get a definitive diagnosis regarding this condition as it may cause aspiration pneumonia.

Another issue around eating well is the condition of the elder's mouth and teeth. Teeth are essential to eating. Missing teeth, poorly fitting dentures, and painful teeth or gums all make eating and swallowing difficult. According to the Advanced Institute for Oral Health, twenty-six percent of all Americans over sixty-five years old have either lost one full arch or all their teeth. The consequence of tooth loss is jawbone loss, and people with dentures are losing bone. Dental implants can stop this condition provided there is enough bone left to hold the implant.[5]

There is no substitute for your own teeth, so good oral hygiene (brushing and flossing daily) plus dental cleanings and check-ups every six-months are essential. Dental check-ups catch problems early, especially in detecting gum disease and tooth decay before they get out of hand. Good dental hygiene combined with eating nutritious foods (low in sugar) all contribute to keeping one's own teeth forever. If an elder is unable to perform the daily oral hygiene regime, caregivers need to be educated on how to assist or perform brushing and flossing for the elder.

Some elders lose interest in eating due to a loss of smell or taste. It is hard to fathom how much smell enhances appetite until one gets a bad cold and realizes that not being able to smell really impacts ones desire for food. It is the same for taste.

SOCIALIZING AROUND A MEAL

Many elders prepare and eat their meals in isolation. This is one of the biggest challenges when caring for an elder who lives alone. Senior centers go a long way to alleviate this during the noon hour by providing a nutritious hot lunch with other seniors. The issue is getting elders to the center if they are no longer driving. Driving an elder to the local senior center can be part of the caregiver's care plan or some local taxi services may give seniors a discounted ride to and from the center.

As you can see, establishing a better quality of life for an elder is many faceted; it takes a consistent team and continuous monitoring of the elder's condition. This may seem daunting at first, but it will pay dividends as time progresses.

TASK LIST

☐ Make sure the elder has a sustainable way to obtain and purchase nutritious food.

☐ Schedule companionship around eating either by using Senior Centers for some meals and scheduled family and friend visits at mealtime.

☐ Maintain good oral health with regular dental visits.

☐ Establish a monitoring system to observe any weight loss or change in condition.

*"I learn by going where
I have to go."*
■ THEODORE ROETHKE

CHAPTER EIGHT
DRIVING

In this Chapter...

- ■ DRIVING AND OUR INDEPENDENCE

- ■ ELDER DRIVING FACTS

- ■ HOW TO PROCEED WITH AN UNSAFE ELDER DRIVER

DRIVING AND OUR INDEPENDENCE

Driving! Americans and their love affair with cars is legendary. It is the teenager's rite of passage into adulthood. Even teens who are failing every subject in school manage to study and pass the written and practical part of the driving test. It is all tied in with our independence and freedom to come and go spontaneously. The cornerstone of our culture is independence and rugged individualism, and the symbol of that independence is the car. Even cities that have good public transportation and offer incentives to carpool, often fail to pry Americans out of their cars.

One can, therefore, understand the extreme resistance to relinquish the car keys when one reaches an age when it is no longer safe to drive. This is perhaps one of the thorniest and most difficult issues to face as one ages. An elder may become angry and resistant when an adult child or friend brings up the issue. Fearing the reaction is one reason families and friends are reluctant to approach the subject. Hopefully, by the end of this chapter, you will have some tools and the courage to take action when and if the need arises.

DETERMINING ELDER DRIVING SAFETY

How does one know when driving is no longer safe for both the elder and the general public? Here are a few indicators:

◀ Has vision and hearing deficits

◀ Exhibits physical decline

◀ Has slowed reflexes

◖ Exhibits medication side effects

◖ Has excessive alcohol consumption

◖ Has diagnosis as Alzheimer's, Parkinson's, or strokes

◖ Has received warnings and tickets

◖ Does not notice other vehicles honking

◖ Asks passengers for navigational assistance

◖ Becomes lost or confused in familiar territory

◖ Bumps into other cars or other close calls

◖ Becomes confused and angry when driving

◖ Drives too slowly

◖ Misjudges distances

◖ Sees with difficulty at night

◖ Accidentally hits the gas pedal instead of the brakes

◖ Forgets to buckle up

◖ Does not stop at stop signs or lights

◖ Does not see or notice other cars, pedestrians, or cyclists

◖ Makes poor decisions or judgment calls

Here is a perfect example of an elder who drove far too long. My father and mother came to visit me one summer, and they were in their late seventies. I was not aware at the time that my father was impaired in his driving. My father and my teenaged son got in the car to do some errands. My father was not in his familiar territory and went the wrong way on a busy arterial through the city.

His response was, "Why are these crazy fools all going the wrong way?" Fortunately, everyone else slowed down honking as they maneuvered around him. When my son told me later that evening what had happened, I knew that I could no longer allow my Dad to drive in unfamiliar territory. At the very least, he would never be allowed to drive my children or me.

Ideally, elders themselves may know when it is time to give up their car keys. I have had many clients who willingly gave up driving when they knew they were no longer safe drivers. If you are adult children who have aging parents that willingly hang up their keys, express your appreciation and admiration to them! They have just made their life and yours much easier and safer. Self-recognition and family support is crucial in this issue.

ELDER DRIVING FACTS

Here are some facts about elder driving. According to the Insurance Institute for Highway Safety (www.iihs. org),[1] seventy-year-olds and older have higher crash rates per mile than middle-age drivers, but not as many as teen drivers. This crash rate rises significantly in drivers eighty-five and older. Many elders self-limit their driving. For example, they do not drive at night or do not drive during rush hours. Due to the aging boomer generation, however, there will be more older drivers on the road, and they are keeping their licenses longer due to longevity.

There are no easy answers or specific laws when an elder should curtail or stop driving. It is not about a specific age, but more about skills, health, and safety. Some people should stop or curtail driving in their sixties and others not until they are much older. Furthermore, there are no national regulations or laws about license renewals for the elderly. Some states do have regulations for an elder acquiring a license or renewing a license. In some states the elder may have to appear in person to renew a license, or on testing, may be told to curtail their driving, or their license may be revoked due to vision decline or confusion when testing. Physicians may prescribe no driving due to physical decline or medication issues. This is sent to the DMV. In my experience, some elders continue to drive anyway even if their licenses are revoked.

According to an excellent 2013 article in *New Hampshire Magazine*,[2] the current projections from the AAA Foundation for Traffic Safety state by 2025 more than twenty-five percent of drivers will be over sixty-five years old. These drivers do not get into accidents because they are reckless, but because of decline (vision, hearing, stiffness, slow reflexes), and they tend to be more seriously injured or die because of their fragility. This article was chosen because it represents a more rural area of the country and pointed out the necessity of driving for these rural elders. Public transportation is not always available, and stores and services may be some distance away from an elder's home. These factors compel some elders to stay behind the wheel much longer than they should.

Because of all these variables mentioned so far, it is best to deal with the issue of elder driving on an individual basis. According to the New Hampshire article, in order to safely remain behind the wheel as long as possible, get vision and hearing checked on a regular basis, get enough sleep, and monitor medication side effects that may increase driving risks. The AAA Foundation for Traffic Safety states that ninety-five percent of elders take medication that could impair their driving. Keeping the car in top form is vital; this includes overall maintenance and repair, especially of tires and brakes. Ideally, the car should have power steering and brakes, an automatic transmission, and large mirrors. It should be easy to get in and out.

In a 2012 *Slate* article, "Give Me the Keys, Dad," intersections are far more perilous for the elder driver.[3] According to a Traffic Injury Prevention study, intersection crashes caused fifty percent of deaths in accidents involving drivers eighty-five years old or older. Indecision and loss of judgment about whether to safely proceed through the intersection and failure to see another car were cited as reasons for this statistic.

If you want to know what your state's requirement is about acquisition and renewal for an elder's driver's license, go to www.iihs.org and click on older drivers and then on state laws. You will get a listing of all states and their requirements.[4]

HOW TO PROCEED WITH AN UNSAFE ELDER DRIVER

Before doing anything, I strongly suggest AARP's excellent multimedia presentation, "We Need to Talk."[5] Take the time to go through this presentation. It will take over an hour, but it is well worth it. It will give you an understanding of what giving up the car keys means to the elder driver as well as compassionate action to take when met with resistance.

There are two levels of unsafe driving. One is minor and the other is major and very unsafe.

Level One signs. Level one signs may be the elder sometimes hits a curb or puts on the left turn signal when he is turning right. He has not had any accidents, and he is not putting himself or others in immediate danger.

◀ Take action and talk with the elder. These conversations should be frequent and can cover general topics like rising gas prices, cost of car maintenance, crowded road conditions.

◀ Hopefully you have watched the AARP presentation and can talk respectfully and compassionately to the elder.

◀ Discuss how other elders you know have curtailed or given up driving.

◀ Regularly monitor and observe how the elder is driving. Ride along. (Do not discuss driving issues while the elder is behind the wheel.) Write down any issues and the date for later conversations. Is this a consistent pattern?

◀ The talk should center on health and safety, not around age.

◀ Plan ahead! Talk at first signs of a driving issue.

◀ Encourage her to take an elder driving safety program, as AARP provides. These are held in local hospitals and senior centers.

◀ Cars should be well maintained, easy to drive, and fit the elder's body. It is stunning to see an elder driver whose seat is so low, she can barely see over the steering wheel.

◀ Listen! Allow the elder to express his concerns and what driving means to them. Validate his feelings.

◀ Suggest a driving assessment. This is done by occupational therapists who are certified to do this. Your local hospital may provide this service through their rehab department or through clinics. According to the American Occupational Therapy Association,[6] this valuable service costs between $250.00 to $500.00 and takes about two hours. These professionals want to make the elder safe and successful while driving, so it is not just about stopping an elder from driving. Occasionally, they may make that recommendation, but more often than not, they make recommendations that assist the elder to be safer. To find a therapist or center that provides these assessments, go to www.aota.org and click on their online database to find the nearest service.

◀ Accompany the elder to her physician to talk about driving. Make sure the elder is not taking medications that may seriously impair her driving. The physician can send an order to the DMV requesting that the elder be summoned for a driving assessment or may simply write a prescription to curtail or cease driving. Sometimes that is enough inducement for the elder to comply.

◀ It may be that curtailing driving in some way decreases the risk: for example, not driving at night or not driving during rush hours or not driving on freeways. Most elders, themselves, curtail driving in these circumstances.

Level Two signs. Level two signs are much more serious and threaten to be harmful to the elder, their passengers, and the general public. Signs that Level One driving has now progressed to Level Two driving include changes in health, physical decline, medications affecting alertness and judgment, cognitive decline, near misses, getting lost in familiar places, and actual car crashes. At this level, the elder should not drive.

◀ Take action without delay! Select someone in the elder's life whom the elder respects and trusts. This may be an adult child, a faith leader, a physician, or a close friend. Hopefully, conversations about driving have been occurring on an ongoing basis. If this is about changing health or medications, involve the physician.

◀ It is more respectful to talk about the elder "hanging up the keys," instead of, "we will take away the keys."

◀ Listen! Hear in the elder's voice his anger and resentment. Validate those feelings.

◀ Ask the elder how she would feel if she had an accident that injured or killed another passenger or another driver such as a mother or father and children.

◀ Offer alternative transportation, which may include family, friends, public transportation, taxis, and something called Independent Transportation Networks, which will be discussed later. The Hartford Company identifies alternate transportation, how much that will cost, and how to find that in specific areas of the country. It is imperative that alternate means of transportation including family support be established ahead of time. These conversations take planning and preparation. Leaving an elder with no transportation alternative can lead to isolation, depression, and anger.

◀ Remain positive. Explain how much the elder will save by not owning a car and how that saved money can be used to pay for alternate transportation.

◀ If all else fails, you may have to take measures like disabling the car, filing down or removing the keys, towing away the car. This is a last resort, however, and hopefully the other measures will work.

◀ If a license has been revoked and somehow the elder has found a way to continue driving, you can call your local police department and report an unsafe driver driving without a license.

◀ In rural areas where alternatives to transportation are not available, it may mean a move to a town or city that provides these alternatives, a move near family who can provide support, or to an elder facility or community that provides transportation.

◀ Hiring agency caregivers to provide transportation is another option. If the elder is compliant with not driving, the caregiver can drive the client's car, which decreases the cost. If the caregiver must use a personal vehicle, there is a cost per mile on the bill.

Independent Transportation Networks (www.itnameri-ca.org) are non-profits that match seniors with volunteer drivers providing door-to-door service in ITN vans. Riders are encouraged to make a donation if they can. In Seattle, there are no ITN chapters, but there is a non-profit senior driving service called Hyde Shuttles which performs the same service in the greater Seattle area (phone 206-727-6262, www.seniorservices.org/transportation/HydeShuttles.aspx).

To see if such a service exists in your area, go to www.itnamerica.org and look at their interactive map to find a service in your area. If you do not see an ITN service in your area, go to your local senior services site and click on transportation. With all of these services, you need to plan ahead and call at least twenty-four to forty-eight hours in advance to reserve your trip. This takes away the spontaneity of getting in your own car and going on the spur of the moment. This loss takes some transition time.

As you can see, this can get complicated. It may take a lot of planning and conversation, but it is an issue that cannot be ignored or swept under the rug. The risks are too great.

STORY: TAKING AWAY THE CAR, GRADUALLY

 Some years ago I was involved with a patient who had a diagnosis of moderate Alzheimer's. He was driving daily. When I visited him in his home for the admission visit, it was clear at that time he should not be driving. The family had been trying to get him to stop driving but had consistently been met with anger and denial.

It was one of the reasons they called for help from an elder care manager. I also broached the subject with this elder and was met with the same response. Getting back to the office, I requested a case conference with our director and other care managers. We finally came up with a plan to recommend to the family, which was as follows:

❶ We would provide a daily caregiver for eight hours a day, and she would do all the driving in her car, keeping his daily routine the same.

❷ The car keys to the client's car would be locked in a box unknown to the client.

❸ When the elder looked for the keys, the caregiver would offer to drive him wherever he needed to go.

The family agreed to start with this plan. The first day went well, but we encountered resistance on the second day. The elder produced another set of keys, took the car, and went before the caregiver could stop him. We proceeded to plan B.

We instructed the family to disable the car. When the elder went to start the car, it would not start. The elder then called his mechanic to come get the car and fix it. We instructed the family to call the mechanic and tell him to keep the car for a while. Now there was only the caregiver's car. With the elder's car and keys now gone, he had to depend on the caregiver. He gradually over the next two weeks became acclimated to this new way of transportation (plus companionship) and settled into a routine. He never mentioned his car again. This may seem extreme to some of you, but it is far better than having an impaired elder not only injure themselves but also injure some other innocent party.

Many elder needs can be met by delivery systems. Some drug stores will deliver medications. Some grocery stores will deliver groceries ordered either over the phone or online. It is imperative that driving retirement does not cause the elder to become shut in and deprived of all socialization. Transportation to social events and outings with friends needs to be maintained. It may, in some instances, be necessary for an elder to move nearer to services and transportation. Taking away driving privileges without putting an alternative plan in place can be disastrous for the well-being of the elder.

TASK LIST

- ☐ Watch the AARP "We Need to Talk" presentation.

- ☐ Start the conversation with the elder as soon as issues occur. This may take many conversations.

- ☐ Get physician involved. Check medications, and get vision/hearing checked.

- ☐ Keep elder's car in top running condition and make sure car fits the elder.

- ☐ Take interim action like not driving after dark and not driving during peak hours.

- ☐ If level 1 driving progresses to level 2, take immediate action.

- ☐ Do not ignore driving issues hoping nothing will happen.

"Now for some heart work."
■ Rainier Maria Rilke

MANAGING ALCOHOL USE DISORDER

Alcohol abuse is one of the least understood, under diagnosed, and under treated conditions in the elderly. It causes chaos on a number of levels from causing frequent falling, to medication interactions, to impaired judgment and confusion, to alcohol specific disorders, (cirrhosis of the liver) to worsening of health conditions, suicide, and others. It is often difficult to diagnose, as the symptoms of alcohol abuse are similar to other age related symptoms such as memory loss, fatigue, and mood changes.[1] Many elders are resistant to treatment as they do not want to think of themselves as addicted.

According to a national 2008 survey done by the National Institute on Alcohol Abuse and Alcoholism, forty percent of adults age sixty-five and older, drink alcohol.[2] Although alcohol use disorder (AUD) seems to decline with age, it is still the most frequently abused substance in the elderly and is rising due to the boomer bubble and longevity.

The literature on the elder and alcohol divide the population with AUD into two categories — early onset drinkers and late onset drinkers. Early onset drinkers (two-thirds) have drunk alcohol since an early age in their twenties and thirties, and generally show declining health and chronic health conditions more than the late onset drinkers. Late onset drinkers (one-third) start drinking in their elder years due to major life events and losses such as loss of a devoted spouse.[3]

In the past ten years or more, there has been new thinking and research into alcohol abuse. Instead of using the old terms such as alcoholic, and addicted, problematic drinking is now called alcohol use disorder or AUD, and there are new treatment modalities, concepts, and new medications that make managing AUD more successful than in the past. Elders are now being taught to manage their drinking and may not have to totally stop. Others will need to stop if addicted to ever increasing amounts of alcohol. It is now accepted that people may have to try several times or more to stop. It is a process and no longer a failure if you try and are not successful. You simply try again. The good news is that elders can be successful in managing their AUD or stopping, given the newer treatment concepts of medication and cognitive therapy, especially group therapy with their own age group. Alcohol use disorder is now considered a chronic care management issue just as managing heart disease, asthma, hypertension, and other chronic conditions of aging.[4]

WHY IS ALCOHOL AN ISSUE IN THE ELDERLY?

When it comes to alcohol, elders are at special risk, as our bodies change as we age when it comes to metabolizing alcohol. Our metabolism (the process by which our bodies use food and water to grow and produce energy) slows and thus alcohol stays in our bodies longer. Tolerance to alcohol is reduced, putting the elder at risk for falls, car accidents, and other injuries. In addition, alcohol and medications common to elders often do not mix. Alcohol can also exacerbate certain diseases or symptoms such as cardiac conditions, diabetes, cognition symptoms, memory issues, and hypertension. Alcohol can place added stress on a liver that is already working hard to process the medications common to the elder.

Even a small amount of alcohol in the elderly can impair judgment, coordination, and reaction time, which may lead to falls, accidents, and automobile crashes. According to the National Institutes of Health, alcohol is involved in sixty percent of fatal burn injuries, drowning, and homicides. Alcohol is involved with forty percent of fatal car crashes, fatal falls, and suicide. The rate of hip fractures in older adults rises with drinking alcohol. Elder driving and drinking increases the rate of car accidents. Alcohol misuse is also involved with elder abuse (physical, emotional, financial, and neglect), which includes self-neglect as well as neglect by others.[5]

Alcohol in the elderly can play havoc with common medications taken by the elderly and can seriously affect the expected outcomes for certain medications.

Medications that do not mix with alcohol are as follows:

■ Aspirin or non-steroidal anti-inflammatory drugs like Ibuprofen. Alcohol increases risk of stomach bleeding when paired with these medications.

■ Tylenol (acetaminophen) taken with alcohol can cause liver damage.

■ Cold and allergy medications (antihistamines) that cause drowsiness plus alcohol can further increase drowsiness and mental or physical impairment. This can lead to falls and accidents.

■ Cough syrup that contains alcohol combined with additional alcoholic drinks causes impairment leading to falls and accidents.

■ Sleeping aids, anti-depressants, anti-anxiety medications, and pain relievers plus alcohol cause many symptoms, including memory problems, excessive drowsiness, and rapid heartbeat.

■ Medications for high blood pressure, diabetes, cardiac conditions, and gout combined with alcohol may worsen these conditions.[6]

HOW MUCH ALCOHOL IS TOO MUCH?

In order to answer that question, it is necessary to define what comprises a drink. There are many resources for this question and they all state much the same thing. One drink is equal to the following:

◀ One 12-ounce can or bottle of beer, ale, or wine cooler

◀ One 8 or 9 ounce can or bottle of malt liquor

◀ One 5-ounce glass of red or white wine

◀ One 1.5 ounce shot glass of hard liquor like gin or vodka

Do not count on the glass or container to guide you. Wine glasses are now the size of small bowls holding three times or more of what wine glasses used to hold. A five-ounce glass of wine is just a little more than half a measuring cup. Pouring a half cup of wine into a wine "bowl" will make it look like you are just getting a tablespoon prompting you to pour much more.

GUIDELINES FOR ELDERS AND DRINKING ALCOHOL

Elders who are over sixty-five years old and do not take medications should not have more than three drinks a day and no more than seven drinks a week. Elders with health issues who are on medications may need to drink less or not at all.[7]

Always inform your physician of your alcohol intake and ask your physician if you may drink alcohol with your disease condition and medications. Your physician will inform you of any issues with alcohol and your disease and medications, and may even adjust your medications accordingly. Your pharmacist is also a source of information about your medications and alcohol, and your medications may even come with a warning on the bottle about not mixing a particular medication with alcohol. Over-the-counter medications also have warnings about not mixing the medication with alcohol. Be sure to heed these warnings.

INDICATORS THAT THERE COULD BE AN AUD ISSUE

Answering "yes" to any one of the following questions may indicate a drinking problem:

- Have you ever felt you should decrease your drinking?

- Are you ever annoyed because people talk about your drinking?

- Do you feel guilty when you drink?

◀ Do you ever drink first thing in the morning to steady yourself or for any other reason?

If you answered, "yes" to just one of these questions, talk with your physician and get help if alcohol is interfering with your life, your relationships, and your health.[8]

GETTING HELP

The good news is people can be successfully treated. This is due to the newer concepts, newer treatments, and medications. There are many things you can do to help change your drinking.

❶ You can start tracking how much alcohol you are getting in each drink and how many drinks you are having each day.

❷ Plan how many days in a week you want to drink. Plan some days without a drink.

❸ Pace and space. Do not drink more than one drink in an hour. Have a non-alcoholic drink like water, juice, and soda between alcoholic drinks.

❹ Have something to eat while drinking.

❺ Remove alcohol from the home.

❻ Avoid alcohol when angry or upset.

PLAN AHEAD

❶ Participate in interests that do not involve alcohol.

❷ Avoid people, places, and time of day that make you want to drink.

❸ Plan something else to do if you feel an urge to drink.

❹ Practice saying "no thank you" when offered a drink and ask for a non-alcoholic option.

❺ Remind yourself how important it is to be healthy so you can enjoy the things you like doing or for your grandchildren.[9]

Seek help from your physician who will guide you to the best treatment option. Most people need a combination of treatments such as medications, meeting on a regular basis with a substance abuse counselor, joining a support group for elder clients, and receiving support from family and friends. It has been well documented that elders are more successful if they join a support group in their age range rather than mixed in with youth and young adults.

Alcoholics Anonymous (AA) and their twelve-step program is open to anyone who is willing to stop drinking. Here are some resources in addition to your physician.

Your local health department.

Alcoholics Anonymous (AA). Look up Alcoholics Anonymous in your local phone book. AA's main office: Grand Central Station P.O. Box 459 New York, NY 10163 Phone: 1-212-870-3400; web site: www.aa.org

Al-Anon. Look up Al-Anon in your local phone book or call 1-888-425-2666 (toll-free) to find a meeting for family and friends of the elder. Al-Anon's main office: 1600 Corporate Landing Parkway Virginia Beach, VA 23454 Phone: 1-757-563-1600; web site: www.al-anon.alateen.org

Eldercare Locator. Contact this service to ask about resources near you. Phone: 1-800-677-1116 (toll-free); web site: www.eldercare.gov

Substance Abuse and Mental Health Services. When you call this toll-free number, a recorded message gives you the following choices: get a referral to local substance abuse treatment, speak with someone about substance abuse treatment, and ask for printed material on alcohol or drugs. Phone: 1-800-662-4357 (toll-free); web site: www.samhsa.gov

The main thing is to stay with the effort to either curtail your drinking or to stop. Keep trying. It may take more than one or two attempts.

FAMILY SUPPORT TO MANAGE DRINKING

Steps to take if you suspect an elder is over-using alcohol:

- The first thing to do is speak to the elder and ask. If done in a quiet, calm, compassionate manner, most elders will at least respond in some way. It may take several conversations, but keep at it.

- Speak to the primary care physician who may give the elder a screening test to ascertain alcohol use. The physician may initiate a discussion with the elder and family as to their awareness and willingness to treat. The physician may also adjust medications, knowing that alcohol is playing a part in the elder's medications and health issues.

- Participate if a confrontation is needed.

- Assist in coordination with community services at home.

- Provide support during detox and chronic treatment.

- Make decisions for older alcoholics with impaired cognition who are unable to process information, weigh consequences, or communicate decisions.

- The main goal is to keep the elder safe. This may mean to limit or stop driving. With physician permission, dilute bottles by a third and then by a half.

- If the elder is malnourished, initiate a nutrition consultation.

- Initiate a personal trainer for the elder and establish an exercise program to do at home.

- Decrease isolation and increase socialization.[10]

An elder care manager may be called by the adult children to intervene with an elder who is drinking and is now a danger to themselves and/or to others. The family may even be estranged from the elder, having given up a long time ago trying to deal with this problem.

STORY: ALCOHOL ABUSE #1

 I received a call from a son who had long ago given up on his father but now was extremely anxious as his eighty-five-year-old father was drinking heavily and driving. The father had many recent fender benders in his neighborhood, going on errands and getting

alcohol. Many of these accidents were one-car accidents running into trees as the father lived in a forest-
ed area. Fortunately, no one else had been involved or
had been hurt, but the son felt it was only a matter of
time.

When I went to do an assessment and admit this elder to services, I found James in a drunken stupor barely able to stand up. According to a friend who arrived
at the house with me, this man often just collapsed on
the stairs going to his bedroom on the second story
and slept on the stairs until morning. This had been a
lifetime of abuse, and family members were no longer
involved in any way including a wife and two sons.
This was one of the hardest cases I had ever managed,
but we did make progress.

After the son accepted the assessment with recommendations, we started to put the plan in place. The
first thing we did was to provide a caregiver 24/7 to
care for this elder in his home. James was extremely
resistant; he wanted no one to interfere with his life.
At times we had to instruct the caregiver to stay in
their car until James's temper fits subsided. Gradually
over time, he came to accept the caregivers who were
preparing nutritious and delicious meals, which was a
change for James. He also began to gradually enjoy the
companionship.

His physician was heavily involved once the physician could see some progress. We were given physician
approval to gradually dilute the alcohol with physician
monitoring. Medications were added to reduce James's
cravings. A routine was established in which the caregiver drove him to his former activities. Unfortunately,
his car had to be disabled and taken away, but by that
time, James had accepted the caregivers who were
driving him everywhere. A sleep routine was established
over time and with decreased alcohol intake, nutritious
meals, a daily exercise regime, companionship and

socialization, this man was finally living a quality of life he had not had in a long time. It was not a smooth road to get to this point, and many times I thought we would not make it. He was still an irascible and at times, a volatile old man, but he continued to make progress with his alcoholism up until his death. This case took the time and skills of many people and also took estate resources that most people do not have.

STORY: ALCOHOL ABUSE, #2

 Elizabeth was an elderly widow, who lived alone, and she called the elder care management company for some help "every once in awhile." On doing the assessment, I was almost sure alcohol was a factor. Unknown liquids had spilled and stained the carpet, the wall in back of the oven was scorched, a teapot had the bottom burned out, and the refrigerator was nearly empty. I kept looking for bottles of alcohol but could not find any. Elizabeth herself denied use of alcohol except "for an occasional drink." On my second visit, I could definitely smell alcohol on her person and asked her if she had been drinking. Smiling, she waved her hand airily, and said I must be smelling her new perfume.

I noticed new bruises on her head that were not there on my first visit. When I asked about these, she again just dismissed these as just a minor fall. Fortunately during my visit, she excused herself to use the bathroom. Elizabeth spent most of her time in her upstairs bedroom so I felt that the alcohol was somewhere in her room. While she was gone, I quickly looked around pulling up the bedspread to look under the bed. Packed tight underneath the bed were countless bottles of alcohol.

When Elizabeth returned from the bathroom, I confronted her with the alcohol. She laughed saying,

"I have been busted." She had been falling regularly, and six months previously had been hospitalized
for a broken wrist secondary to a fall. She had lost
her husband of many years one year previous to my
visit. As a couple, they had fallen into a routine of
going to the local bars every afternoon and having a
"rollicking good time," as Elizabeth put it, on a daily
basis. Now that her husband was gone, Elizabeth had
become a reclusive shut-in at home. Not only was
she deprived of any socialization, but she was also
losing weight as she was drinking her calories instead
of eating nutritious food. She "hated" eating alone
as she put it, and just was not hungry. In the past six
months, she had been hospitalized twice for pneumonia and when I listened to her lungs, her breathing sounded moist.

The first thing was to get her respiratory condition
addressed. The physician was reluctant to make another
appointment as she had broken so many appointments
without notice. I assured him we would be there. On
taking her to that appointment, the pneumonia was
indeed not resolved and antibiotics were prescribed.
Permission was given to dilute the alcohol gradually
over time. Caregivers were hired to provide safety monitoring and fall prevention, but also to fix nutritious
meals and provide companionship. The bottles were
cleared out from under the bed and put in the kitchen
where the caregivers had access to the supply and could
dilute as instructed.

Part of the care plans included daily walks and
exercise. Caregivers were driving her to senior center activities which provided a whole new venue for
socialization instead of the bar scene. Like James, she
never became completely sober, but her life did change
for the better, and she enjoyed a much healthier quality
of life. Elizabeth had never had children and had no
other living family members. Eventually the caregiving

hours increased to 24/7 as she became frail. She did not fall again due to safety measures put in place, and her respiratory condition was completely resolved. She continued to live a quality life in her home for several more years with caregivers in attendance until she died.

You may be wondering why the alcohol is not taken completely away and the elder is told to attend an alcohol cessation program like Alcoholics Anonymous. If the elder is willing and able, that would certainly be a good plan; however, in my experience, elders are usually not willing to give up alcohol. They have been drinking literally for decades and see no reason to stop at "this late stage of my life." If you start focusing on the alcohol issue, everything else gets put on a back burner. If the alcohol can be controlled so it is not a safety issue and is not interfering with medications, you have perhaps accomplished a favorable outcome and can move on to other issues.

MEDICATION ABUSE

Drug abuse in the elderly usually involves overuse of medications such as pain medicines and other over-the-counter medicines rather than illegal drugs, although, that also can be a factor. Medication abuse is hard to diagnose, especially if the elder is reluctant or refuses to reveal a drug problem. One of the most important things an elder care manager or family caregiver does is organize and update an elder's medication regime in partnership with the physician. Often pain is poorly controlled and elders take whatever medications they perceive will relieve their pain. With tighter physician and care management control over medications combined with prescribing the correct medication for the pain source, many elders may enjoy an improvement in their pain level. Resolution of pain is one of the top priorities for a care manager.

This does not always mean medications are a solution. Some pain conditions may be alleviated with a round of physical therapy, exercise, therapy pools, massage, relaxation techniques, pain support groups, meditation, and other modalities. Ask your physician to prescribe these alternatives some of which may be reimbursed by Medicare or Medicaid.

In summary, alcohol and drug abuse is a particularly difficult problem to work with, but with patience, physician involvement, good care management, and caregiver assistance, the quality of life for the elder may be greatly increased.

TASK LIST

☐ TALK TO THE ELDER ABOUT THEIR AUD AND KEEP TALKING.

☐ INVOLVE THE PHYSICIAN AND FOLLOW RECOMMENDATIONS.

☐ RECOGNIZE THE IMPORTANCE OF FAMILY SUPPORT AND INTERVENTION.

☐ USE A CARE MANAGER TO PROVIDE ONGOING MONITORING AND SUPPORT.

☐ TAKE ADVANTAGE OF COMMUNITY SUPPORT SERVICES.

CHAPTER TEN

DEMENTIA SYMPTOMS AND ALZHEIMER'S DISEASE

In this Chapter...

- ■ DEALING WITH DEMENTIA

- ■ STAGES OF ALZHEIMER'S DISEASE

- ■ ALZHEIMER'S DISEASE CARE STRATEGIES

- ■ PLANNING FOR THE COST OF ALZHEIMER'S

DEALING WITH DEMENTIA

Over the years of working with elders, I will often ask them what is their worst fear about growing old? The answer comes shooting out of their mouths without a second thought: "Losing my mind!" They do not ponder and hesitate before answering. It is not about losing their spouse of fifty years or even fear of death. In fact, most of them say they do not fear death, but *do* fear what may lead up to death. A number of people will also add that they fear unresolvable pain, as they grow older, but it is a distant second compared to losing one's mind. I have played this scenario over and over, and it does not change. This is the main fear for all of us as we age, and every little "senior moment" or difficulty recalling a name or word sends us into a fear state that we may be getting Alzheimer's.

Dementia comes from Latin and means *without a mind*. It is not a diagnosis but a series of symptoms as follows:

◀ Memory loss, usually short term memory loss

◀ Difficulty with language. Can't find the right word or recall a name.

◀ Problems performing everyday tasks such as personal care.

◀ Disorientation as to time and place.

◀ Poor judgment and decision making.

◀ Issues with abstract thinking.

◀ Consistently misplacing items.

◀ Changes in mood and behavior.

- Personality changes.
- No initiative or motivation.[1]

These symptoms may be caused by a variety of diagnoses or conditions:

- Medication side effects or interactions
- Nutritional deficiencies
- Depression
- Alcohol abuse
- Vascular dementia
- Strokes
- Parkinson's
- Brain tumors
- Infections
- Head injuries
- Various chronic illnesses
- Electrolyte imbalance
- Alzheimer's disease
- Lewy Body Dementia
- Pick's disease

Some of these conditions are reversible such as depression, nutritional deficiencies, and medication side effects and interactions.

I could always tell when my mother was getting a urinary infection (for which she was prone) because she would become very confused and out of it. When she had her stroke, she was standing in the middle of the street talking with neighbors and suddenly said, "I do not know the way home." My father turned to her and said, "You are standing right in front of your home." My mother just wandered off. My father got her to the hospital immediately where her stroke was treated in a timely manner.

Any sudden change in condition resulting in confusion or loss of function means an immediate 911 call. *Time lost is brain lost* when it comes to a stroke. My mother's confusion and depression following her stroke became worse, but then gradually lessened. This is why it is so important to have a physician assess these symptoms before jumping to any conclusions. You may also want to get a second opinion.

In a September/October 2008 AARP magazine article, "Why Doctors Make Mistakes," an example is given about a misdiagnosis of dementia symptoms.[2] An elderly woman had been diagnosed with Alzheimer's disease. Due to her worsening symptoms and fading memory, the family was searching for a nursing home, but decided to get a second opinion from a neurologist. This woman did not have Alzheimer's, but was suffering from anemia and vitamin B-12 deficiency, which causes dementia symptoms. Do not assume it is just old age and then do nothing about it. Take action.

Usually, however, dementia symptoms indicate a "slow progressive loss of mental functions, including memory, thinking, judgment, and ability to learn, eventually keeping people from performing normal daily activities."[3]

Another term to define is the disease called Alzheimer's, named after the German psychiatrist and neuropathologist who first identified the disease in 1906. Alzheimer's disease is a progressive, irreversible brain illness with increasing dementia whose cause and treatment continue to evade scientists. Usually people with this disease die in four to six years but many may live longer. Alzheimer's usually occurs in people who are over age sixty-five with an increase in people over eighty years of age; however, it may rarely occur in younger people.

Probable causes have been as diverse as aluminum cooking pans to the chemicals in deodorants. Suggested preventions have included maintaining an ideal weight, exercise, losing belly fat, eating Omega 3s, eating deep colorful produce, drinking only decaf drinks, and keeping one's mind active by learning new things. These preventive measures are all healthy and good things to achieve, but there is no guarantee they will prevent Alzheimer's.

In a June, 2009 article for AARP, Maria Shriver, former first lady of California, said this about her father, Sargent Shriver, afflicted with Alzheimer's. "He was the smartest, most literary, actively intellectual, and engaged human being I've ever known, and he got Alzheimer's." When asked if she was afraid of getting Alzheimer's, she replied, "You betcha. Bigtime. I try not to freak out, and I live in the moment." Good advice for all of us. It affects both men and women across all levels of society. If the cause of dementia symptoms is definitely Alzheimer's, then arming yourself with knowledge and making plans for the future is imperative.

When first interacting with families receiving this diagnosis, I make sure they have received the correct diagnosis. I ask them who told them their loved one has Alzheimer's. Not a few people answer they just assumed it was Alzheimer's because their loved one seems confused. They had *not* sought a definitive diagnosis from their primary physician and a neurologist. I urge them to do so as soon as possible.

If they have received this diagnosis from their physician and a neurologist, then I simply spend time listening to them pour out their hearts trying to process this difficult diagnosis. It is everyone's worst nightmare come to fruition. If a family member or the patient has experienced other family members with Alzheimer's, there is real grieving occurring because they know what lies ahead. This diagnosis is heartbreaking and life changing for all involved.

The next thing to do is to link the elder to their local Alzheimer's Association. This invaluable community resource is a lifeline to family members and to the elder. This is not a path to attempt to walk alone. This association provides support groups for family members plus tons of information in easy to read formats. They can assist in finding caregivers and placement facilities.

Alzheimer's support groups are composed of people going through similar experiences as you, and many have found very creative ways of coping with the issues surrounding this diagnosis. You do not feel alone in a support group plus you learn how others are managing the behaviors associated with the disease. Perhaps most of all, you will learn to laugh in a support group. There may be tears as well, but there is always some laughter, which goes a long way on this journey.

After the diagnosis is confirmed and you are plugged into community resources like the Alzheimer's Association, it is time to arm yourself with knowledge as to what lies ahead and how you will cope. This book cannot go into all the details of how to deal with this disease, but there are a few important things to know.

STAGES OF ALZHEIMER'S DISEASE

This disease has been staged into early, mid, and late stage categories. These categories are then divided various ways depending on what source you are using for your information. The following is just one example of the staging of Alzheimer's:[4]

Stage 1. Normal function. There is no impairment.

Stage 2. Mild impairment. There may be mild memory impairment but they are not evident in a medical exam or to friends and family.

Stage 3. Mental decline. Friends, co-workers, family may notice decline. Memory issues may be obvious during a medical exam. Memory impairment is evident but there also may be performance issues at work, reading retention declines, and ability to plan or organize is affected.

Stage 4. Moderate mental decline. Short term memory loss is clear cut. Ability to perform arithmetic is affected. Paying bills and managing finances is affected as is planning and organizing. The patient runs on routine and repeats stories. May show signs of depression.

Stage 5. Moderately severe mental decline. Memory decline becomes major issue. Caregivers are required at this point to perform some, but not all ADLs and IADLs. The patient usually knows her name and knows her close loved ones such as children and spouse. Can still maintain social niceties, but is confused.

Stage 6. Severe mental decline. Memory continues to decline and personality may change. Will need extensive help with ADLs. May become incontinent, may have disrupted awake/sleep cycles. May develop difficult behavior symptoms as paranoia, delusions, hallucinations, and compulsiveness. May wander or try to escape. May pace, rock, or move about. At risk for malnutrition and weight loss due to loss of appetite.

Stage 7. Very severe mental decline. This is the final stage and involves inability to speak and full assistance with all ADLs and IADLs. Swallowing may be impaired. Patients reaching this stage are often chair-bound or bedbound and need full assistance with every aspect of their lives. The patient has limited response.

You are now arming yourself with knowledge, and you are getting connected with the community resources. Next, assure the safety of the loved one with Alzheimer's. Refer again to the chapter on safety. These are all items that will help keep your loved one safe. If the Alzheimer patient tends to wander, alarms may have to be placed on the home exits. Call your local county sheriff and police departments to see if they have a wandering program. Many counties across the country have what is called Project Lifesaver. Estimating that almost sixty percent of Alzheimer's patients will wander, this project provides each patient with a one-ounce electronic bracelet that emits a unique radio signal twenty-four hours a day. If a patient wanders, the caregiver calls 911. A rapid response by a trained team initiates a search and rescue by locating the patient's unique radio signal.

ALZHEIMER'S DISEASE CARE STRATEGIES

Decide *how* to care for this loved one and *who* is going to give the care. In the beginning of this illness, it may be possible for a caring spouse and/or family member to provide the care and supervision necessary but *this is not sustainable.* Care needs will increase as this disease progresses. What may have seemed manageable in the beginning will gradually become unmanageable as time goes on. Plan in the very beginning for what lies ahead.

Countless families try to walk the caregiver path alone or with just one person in attendance. This is always a gradual disaster usually resulting in the solo caregiver becoming ill or in some instances dying due to the enormous stress of trying to do this alone. There is such a thing as a documented caregiver fatigue timeline. Depending on which source you use for this timeline, it may vary slightly.

CAREGIVER FATIGUE TIMELINE

This time line is about the caregiver, NOT the elder with Alzheimer's.[5]

1 – 18 MONTHS

◀ Anxious to provide best possible care for loved one

◀ Manages the person with dementia

◀ Maintains house, garden, car

◀ Attends to family relations

◀ Keeps up appearances

◀ Helps person with dementia through social situations

◀ Remains optimistic, caring, supportive

◀ Operates as superwoman/superman

◀ Attends to personal care

AT 21 MONTHS

◀ Begins to take medication, usually for sleep/ headaches

◀ It becomes harder and harder to keep on top of things

◀ Some help from family may still be available

AT 24 – 32 MONTHS

◀ Emotional and physical resources drained

◀ Less and less contact with personal doctor, dentist, minister, friends

◀ Experiences feelings of powerlessness

◀ Caregiving consumes the day and night

◀ Outside help dwindles away

AT 32 MONTHS

◀ Stress becomes harder to conceal

◀ Caregiver begins taking tranquilizers

◀ Begins using medication for musculoskeletal pain

◀ Sleep is continually disturbed

◀ Caregiver becomes irritable

◀ Less and less contact with others

AT 38 MONTHS

◀ Caregiver feels unhealthy

◀ Finds it hard to get up

◀ Never feels rested

◀ May have hypertension/colitis

◀ Has symptoms of chronic fatigue

◀ Caregiver loses the will to take care of themselves

◀ Is unable to manage the household

◀ Rarely socializes with others

◀ Feels helpless, guilty, a failure

AFTER 50 MONTHS

◀ Has chronic state of fatigue

◀ Caregiver is in a state of unwellness

◀ Is unable to ask for help

◀ Becomes isolated

◀ Is unable to access resources for information or help

This timeline is painful to watch. Even if money is not available for paid caregivers, there are things you can do to alleviate caregiver fatigue. When Nancy Reagan was caring for Ronald Reagan, she gave a very poignant interview about caregiving. She said she was the lucky one, as she could afford skilled and non-skilled caregivers around the clock allowing her to be a loving spouse without the burden of full-time caregiving. She stated she did not know how people cared for their loved ones without help.

It is unfortunate in our country that there is not some financial assistance available, but there are resources and methods that can be of enormous help for the patient, caregivers, and family members. This is *not* the time to be staunchly independent and think you can be superwoman/superman. This *is* the time to reach out to others and to the community at large for all the help you can find. This may be a long road and like any long road, you need to pace yourself with assistance from a supportive team.

A WELL-ORGANIZED PLAN

For anyone dealing with this illness, the following is a set of instructions to put in place in an organized fashion as soon as possible.[6] Do *not* wait until things become so bad that the caregiver is hanging on by his fingernails.

Assemble a caregiving team. First all family members need to sit down and have a family meeting to face this diagnosis and draw up a care plan. This care plan may include the participation of family members, friends, neighbors, and faith community members including the faith leader. It

will also include who is going to do what and how
future care needs will be paid for. Ask people for
their time and talents. Many people are just waiting
to be asked, but will not volunteer unless asked.
Try to spread the work and tasks over many people.
Neighbors can do grocery shopping or come in and
do laundry. Volunteers from a faith community
can come into the home and be a companion for
a couple hours while the caregiver takes some time
off. Long distance family members can contribute
even a small amount of money to defray costs of
caregivers or a housecleaner. It may help to create a
chart or calendar with the tasks to be accomplished
and the frequency. You can then fill in the chart with
the people that will assist in performing each task for
that week.

Access Community Resources. Along with
the Alzheimer's Association resources, another
community resource is adult day care. This
valuable resource takes the elder for the better part
of a day and provides a safe, caring, and gently
stimulating environment for the elder. It is staffed by
trained people caring for the demented elder. Some
day care facilities actually provide transportation
to and from the day care. Many of these facilities
operate on a sliding fee scale. Other community
resources are volunteer bill payers and tax assistance
programs. Contact your county Area Agency on
Aging (AAA) to see if they have a county resource
web site or a booklet listing the senior resources for
your community.

Join a support group. You will find strength in numbers and laughter. You will learn a lot and benefit from the creative ways others have found to cope.

Memory aids. Keep a large calendar for the elder, listing each day's activities. Provide simple written instructions. Put an ID bracelet on the elder or contact Project Lifeline for wandering issues. Create a daily routine or care plan and stick with it. In terms of a demented elder wandering, there are some newer systems on the market that you may want to consider other than ID bracelets and the police/sheriff wandering program. One of these programs is called Comfort Zone and Comfort Zone Check, which is a GPS system that tracks where elders may be if they wander outside of a preset safety zone. The cost starts at $40.00 per month. Check out the Comfort Zone web site or call 1-877-ALZ-4850.[7]

Address Home Safety. See the chapter on safety. In addition, you may want to use an intercom system or baby monitor system. Put a sticker on the phone with emergency numbers.

Educate yourself. Gain knowledge about the disease and how to give compassionate care.

Making the ADLs easier. Allow the elder to be as independent as he is able and use the equipment that makes these tasks easier like a bath bench, hand-held shower, and grab bars. Use volunteers for some of the IADLs such as house cleaning, grocery shopping, transportation, and bill paying.

Remember the importance of socialization and fun. Both the elder and the caregivers need time for socialization, fun, laughter, physical activity, hobbies, outings, etc.

Comply with medication regime. Set up a system for the proper dispensing of medications. See "Taking Medications Correctly" on page 74.

Establish a point person to communicate with your health care providers. Select one person to set up the communication lines with the elder's physicians. Consult a physician for any change in the elder's condition. Do not wait to see what happens or assume that it is nothing to worry about. Any change means a call to the physician.

Make sure there is an emergency plan in place. See the chapter on safety. Always keep the PHR up-to-date and accessible.

Store any dangerous items out of reach. These include hazardous substances, guns, knives, and power tools.

Take care of yourself. This can mean different things to each individual caregiver. I always ask family caregivers what they enjoyed before they assumed the demanding role of caregiving. One man said he enjoyed a twice-weekly game of golf with his friends but had stopped due to the demands of caregiving for his demented spouse. After a brief discussion, we came up with a plan to resume those golf games. He really just needed permission to find a solution, as he was consumed by guilt whenever he left his wife. Arrange for respite assistance. No one can do this 24/7! Get enough sleep and eat nutritiously. Maintain a sense of humor. Pace yourself.

Make sure all documents are in order and up-to-date. See the chapter on documents.

Watch out for depression. Depression is common among caregivers. Seek help immediately from your physician if you notice the signs and symptoms of depression. Access sources of help and support such as faith communities and other community resources.

Guilt. Guilt comes with the territory when caring for someone with Alzheimer's. You feel guilty for not doing more, for getting fatigued, for feeling angry, and at times for wishing the parent or partner would just die. Talk with someone about these feelings, such as your physician, faith leader, Alzheimer's support group, or counselor/therapist.

For those families with financial resources, paid agency caregivers from the very beginning are highly recommended. In the beginning, the elder diagnosed with dementia or Alzheimer's may be able to safely spend some time alone. A paid caregiver may only be needed for two to four hours a day. The need for more caregiver hours will increase, however, depending on how fast the elder progresses through the disease stages. From the beginning, you need to plan on increasing the caregiving hours as needed.

There is no right or wrong way to plan for the future of an Alzheimer's patient. I have sat with families who are very frank about their abilities or willingness to assume a caregiving role. One wife said this about her husband with Alzheimer's. "I do not want to give up my life to care for my husband for the next five years or longer. I want a caregiver here twenty-four hours a day." To some, this may have seemed heartless and selfish. This is not about judging people's abilities or willingness to do this work. Actually in this particular example, it worked out well. She conducted her own life and also spent quality time with her husband who was well cared for at home by agency caregivers. Others will choose to place their loved one in a long-term care facility and visit, as they are able. Medicare does not pay for this, but Medicaid may in some circumstances. Circumstances may preclude family members from assuming the caregiving role. Do not judge others in regard to their unwillingness to assume the caregiver role. The main goal is for the demented elder to be safe and cared for in a caring and compassionate environment.

There are many books on how to manage the behaviors of an elder with Alzheimer's and other dementias. The Alzheimer's Association will often have a library of such materials for your use. There are a few key principles, however, that may be helpful. This one page sheet is from the Santa Cruz Alzheimer's Association and is called, "The ABCs for the Care of People with Dementia."[8]

A – Agree. Do NOT argue. Have a positive approach and ignore the negative.

B – The Brain is broken. Difficult behaviors are caused by brain damage. Blame the disease, not the person. People with dementia cannot learn new things. People with dementia cannot just "try harder."

C – Calm care. Caregiver behaviors and moods can affect the elder. Calm environment. Simple directions. Kind words. Gentle touch. Respond to the elder's feelings.

D – Distract, redirect, reassure. The best approach is to change the situation. Distraction reduces agitation and anger. Reassurance reduces anxiety.

E – Easy. Make it easy. People with dementia can still do many things. Help patients help themselves.

My favorite book of the many I have read on Alzheimer's is one entitled, *To Hold a Falling Star,* by Betty Baker Spohr. It is honest and forthright, and tells with simplicity and love the journey through Alzheimer's with all the pitfalls, tangled emotions, and problems.

Many people have seen articles or heard about possible treatments for Alzheimer's disease but so far there is no known treatment to stop the disease. There are some medications to slow the progression in the early stages and some medications may ameliorate the behavioral or psychiatric symptoms.

PLANNING FOR THE COST OF ALZHEIMER'S DISEASE

The cost of Alzheimer's disease care is in most cases borne by the family. This involves the cost in the home and in facilities. See the chapter on home care costs and facilities for costs and services. Deciding to move a demented

elder from the home setting to a facility is often a difficult decision for families to make. They feel guilt and
anguish about whether it is the right decision. There are
certain signs that a move to a facility may be needed. For
example, the cost of in-home care may be prohibitive
depending on hours needed. The elder is no longer safe.
The caregiver is no longer able to provide care as care
needs are too great.

Here are brief descriptions of care options and their
approximate cost, which will increase over time.[9]

The average costs for long-term-care in the United
States are as follows: (Remember these costs are largely out of pocket. Medicare does not pay for these types
of services. Long-term care insurance, veterans benefits,
and in some instances Medicaid, may pay some costs.)

■ $214 per day or $78,110 per year for semi-private
room in a skilled nursing facility.

■ $239 per day or $87,000 per year for a private room
in a SNF.

■ $3,477 per month or $41,724 per year for basic
services in an assisted living facility. (These costs
could be more depending on services needed.)

■ $21.00 per hour for a home health aide (assistance
with ADLs).

■ $70.00 per day for adult day care services.

ADULT DAY CARE

Cost varies from state to state, but many are on a sliding scale according to income. Medicaid may assist with
costs for low-income seniors.

IN-HOME CARE

The costs vary widely depending on what care is needed, the hours required, and the skill level needed. Personal care (helping with ADLs) costs approximately $21.00 to $28.00 per hour. Around the clock in-home care costs approximately $18,000 to $24,000 per month. These are agency prices. You may be able to find private caregivers at a decreased rate, but be aware of the risks of hiring privately.

RESIDENTIAL CARE

These include retirement communities, assisted living facilities, skilled nursing facilities, special care units (SCUs) specifically for Alzheimer's patients, and continuous care retirement communities. Costs vary depending on facility and care needed. The national average cost for an assisted living facility is $42,000 per year. For a nursing home it is $78,000 per year for a semi-private room and $87,230 per year for a private room.

Special care units, as mentioned above, are facilities that designate a special area for Alzheimer's disease. There has been an increasing trend to redesign living areas into home-like settings with specially trained care personnel. Some examples of these units can be found at Aegis facilities throughout Washington, California, and Nevada. The concept is to create life neighborhoods with a home setting.

Another example is The Best Friends Approach to Alzheimer's Care as created by Virginia Bell and David Troxel in their book by the same name. This is a life affirming approach built around the values and principles of friendship. There are now established Alzheimer's units using this method.

Teepa Snow, MS, Occupational Therapist, is a master trainer in caring for people with Alzheimer's. Her methods both for facility caregiver personnel and for family members are invaluable. Her excellent web site, www.teepasnow.com, is a wealth of information for families and facilities.

If you are looking for a SCU, ask about the methods used and find out how often the facility caregiving personnel receive mandatory education and training.

RESPITE CARE

This care provides for the caregiver to have a break from caregiving. It can be for overnight or several days depending on the need. The Alzheimer's elder is safely cared for in a facility for a brief period or at home with volunteer help or hired in-home caregivers. The cost would vary depending on the amount of volunteer help, in-home paid caregiving, or facility costs.

HOSPICE CARE

This Medicare/Medicaid service is a federal program that focuses on comfort measures, pain control, and support by a team of professionals during the last six months of life. You do not receive a bill for this service if you are on Medicare/Medicaid or have private insurance with a hospice benefit. Hospice care includes comfort measures and pain management by an RN, counseling from a social worker and a spiritual counselor, respite services, and grief counseling. A home health aide is provided for personal care. You need an order from your physician and a six-month prognosis to initiate hospice care. Most hospice care occurs in the home or a skilled nursing facility. There are a few freestanding hospice facilities in the country and some hospitals have "hospice" beds included within the hospital.

ADDITIONAL COSTS

An Alzheimer's diagnosis means planning carefully for what lies ahead. Do not respond to one crisis after another, which is not a plan. When first diagnosed, sit down and start planning. The following list will allow you to look realistically at your resources and secure the best care possible. Have a family meeting and look at both the elder's resources and the family resources. Include the elder if they are in the early stages and can understand the issues. This is a chance to hear what the elder's wishes are. Both elder and family resources may be needed.[10]

Choosing a care setting can be a daunting task. Ask the elder's physician and faith leader. These two people visit care settings frequently and can be a good source of information.

Some additional costs you may face are:

- Ongoing costs for medical treatment
- Medical equipment costs
- Safety related expenses as home modifications or safety services for a wanderer
- Prescription medications
- Personal care supplies such as incontinent briefs
- Adult day care services
- In-home care services
- Full time residential services

The following list identifies some of the documents you will need. Hopefully you have completed this step. Use professional financial and legal advisers to assist you with financial planning. (See "Documentation" on page 21.)

◀ Bank and brokerage account information

◀ Deed, mortgage papers, or ownership statements (A reverse mortgage may free up considerable resources if the elder owns their home.)

◀ Insurance policies especially long term care policies

◀ Monthly or outstanding bills

◀ Pension and other retirement benefits including VA benefits if applicable

◀ Rental income paperwork

◀ Social security payment information

◀ Stock and bond certificates[11]

FINANCIAL NEEDS AND GOALS

The planning meeting should reveal what financial resources are available and what volunteer resources are available in the family, friends, neighbors, and faith community. Using a calendar, start getting specific as to what tasks can be done by volunteers and family and place these entries on the calendar. If paid caregiving is needed, calculate those costs, and add that to the calendar. Keep in mind that costs and caregiving time required will increase as the disease progresses. In addition to planning for actual care, other financial duties need to be discussed and assigned as follows:

◀ Who will pay bills?

◀ Who will arrange for benefit claims?

◀ Who will make investment decisions?

◀ Who will prepare income tax returns?[12]

If at all possible, get professional financial help during this planning stage. Financial advisors and estate planning attorneys can help you identify financial resources, find tax deductions, and assist in making good investment decisions. Make sure they are qualified in elder care and elder law. The following resources will help you find a financial advisor educated in elder care issues.

◀ Eldercare locator online or 800-677-1116

◀ Financial Planning Association online or call 800-322-4237

◀ National Academy of Elder Law Attorneys online

Here is a quick tip list from the Alzheimer's web site.

■ Make a plan early in the diagnosis phase. Talk about finances and future care issues.

■ Find, organize, and review essential documents.

■ Access professional financial and legal help.

■ Try to estimate costs for the entire disease process.

■ Look at all your options for potential income such as insurance options, work related salary/benefits, and personal property options such as a reverse mortgage.

- ■ Find out if you are eligible for any government programs.

- ■ Find out if you are eligible for any tax breaks.

- ■ Explore what finances are available within the family.

- ■ Plan to use low cost and free community services, when available. The Alzheimer's Association is a wealth of information on community services (www.alz.org).

In summary, the most important thing about the long road through Alzheimer's disease is to provide a safe, compassionate, and caring environment for the demented elder. To do this requires every family member, medical provider, and community resource to work together in a planned and coordinated fashion. There cannot be just one caregiver who bears most of the brunt of caregiving. That is not sustainable and may have disastrous consequences. Being armed with knowledge, support, and a plan makes the coming changes easier to accept and thereby helps to avoid a crisis.

TASK LIST

☐ CONVENE A FAMILY MEETING WHEN DIAGNOSIS IS CONFIRMED TO REVIEW AVAILABLE RESOURCES AND PLAN AHEAD. USE A CARE MANAGER, FINANCIAL ADVISOR, AND ELDER LAW ATTORNEY TO ADVISE YOU.

☐ CONNECT WITH YOUR LOCAL ALZHEIMER'S ASSOCIATION.

☐ PLAN AND IMPLEMENT FOR MORE THAN ONE CAREGIVER FROM THE BEGINNING.

☐ THE MAIN GOAL IS TO HAVE THE ELDER IN A SAFE AND CARING ENVIRONMENT.

☐ AVAIL YOURSELF OF ALL LOW-COST OR FREE COMMUNITY RESOURCES.

"It's loneliness and feeling undervalued that boosts a senior's risk of falling for scams."
■ Peter Lichtenberg of Wayne State University's Institute of Gerontology.

CHAPTER ELEVEN
ELDER ABUSE AND SCAMS

In this Chapter...

■ ELDER ABUSE FACTS

■ RECOGNIZING ELDER ABUSE

■ PROTECTING AGAINST ELDER ABUSE

■ SCAMS

ELDER ABUSE FACTS

Elder abuse is widespread and prevalent across all socioeconomic, gender, racial, and religious boundaries. When first entering elder care management, I was stunned to encounter it so often. It can take many guises and forms. It can be very subtle or extremely flagrant. Abuse can happen from a stranger, a family member, a caregiver, and even in rare cases, an estate or elder care attorney. It can happen in the home setting or in a facility. Abuse may be physical abuse, financial abuse, emotional abuse, sexual abuse, neglect (including self-neglect), social abuse, exploitation, scams or a combination of these. The frail and often demented elders may be afraid to say anything or may not know how to express themselves.

We all can suffer from abuse and scams, but elders are a particularly vulnerable population to scams because of the following:

■ They may have a greater disposable income.

■ They have less debt.

■ They may live alone or in isolated circumstances.

■ No one may be watching their money, including the elder.

■ Loneliness makes them appreciate guests coming to their door or over the phone.

■ Memory loss increases opportunity for scams.

■ They may be looking for something to relieve their chronic disease condition.

■ They may no longer be able to pay bills, which then accumulate.

This all makes them susceptible to scams by con artists and financial abuse from family members.[1] In addition, elders may be reluctant to report abuse including financial abuse, as they fear retaliation, are unable to express themselves, or are embarrassed to report it, especially if the abuse is coming from a family member.

According to the Washington Nursing Commission News,[2] in 1986, there were 117,000 reported cases of all abuse. By 1996, the number had increased to 293,000. In 2000, the total number of reports was 472,813. Some current sources believe that as many as 2.5 million elders are abused annually. According to the National Center on Elder Abuse, Bureau of Justice Statistics for 2014, the average number of elderly abuse cases each year is 2,150,000. Almost 10% of the elderly population will experience some type of abuse. 68% of Adult Protective Services cases involve some type of elder abuse.[3] Although data as to the actual number varies from source to source, this will continue to increase as our aging population increases. It is thought that this represents only the tip of the iceberg, and the actual number is much greater. According to the Administration on Aging, for every reported case of elder abuse, five more go unreported.[4]

According to Sid Kirchheimer in the AARP bulletin dated March 5, 2013, Skip Humphrey (son of Hubert Humphrey, former vice president) leads the Office of Older Americans at the Consumer Financial Protection Bureau. This agency was created in the aftermath of the 2008 economic debacle. Its purpose is to protect older consumers, and monitor banks, lenders, and financial institutions. During the recent financial crisis, Americans fifty-five and older lost forty percent of their net worth. This agency is the only one to target financial elder abuse.[5]

Scam artists steal a documented $3 billion a year from the elder population fifty-five and older, but just one in twenty-five reports these crimes. Humphrey states his goal is to answer two questions. "How do we prevent elder citizens from getting ripped off?" "How do we help them make smart financial decisions as they age?" As a care manager, this is why professional estate and elder law attorneys are needed plus trusted family members to oversee and monitor an elder's monies.[6]

Health professionals are called mandated reporters. In other words, when we see or suspect abuse, we are mandated to report the abuse to Adult Protective Services (APS). That being said, anyone can report elder abuse, and it can be an anonymous report. APS is a state program in every county in the country, and they must investigate any report of suspected abuse. (APS web site: www.napsa-now.org)

STORY: THE INTRUDER

 A long distance nephew called me to check on his aunt who lived alone in a rather isolated location. She was in her nineties and was spry and mentally alert except for some short-term memory loss. After doing an assessment, I found that she was having some issues taking her medications correctly and making her own meals. She no longer drove and had no system by which to get groceries. Her nutrition was compromised, and she was losing weight. As I was making notes and drawing up a care plan, I heard a car drive up and the garage door open. I asked, "Who is that, Sarah?" She replied, "Oh that is Michael. He lives in the garage." Michael had come to her door one day and asked for food, which she readily gave him. A couple days later, he returned and asked if he could live in her garage, as he was homeless. She readily agreed.

Once he was ensconced in her garage, he then offered to get groceries for her but told her he needed her checkbook to buy the things she needed. Large amounts of "groceries" had been bought from her checking account. It was actually what prompted the nephew to call for a care manager; he monitored her checking account and was concerned about the large amounts of money being withdrawn.

I got up from my chair slowly and approached the garage with some trepidation. There was indeed a small tent pitched next to Sarah's car. When I asked Michael why he was there, he said he had Sarah's permission and, "you cannot make me leave." I closed the door, locked it, and called the sheriff. I then called the nephew and explained what had been happening. The sheriff immediately removed Michael.

The nephew arrived at his aunt's home a few days later and took full control of her checkbook and finances. He gratefully accepted care management services and oversight plus initiated caregivers for two hours in the morning and two hours in the afternoon for personal care and meal preparation. Under care management, mediplanners for the medications were initiated, and the caregivers reminded Sarah to take them at the designated times. A regular grocery list and nutrition plan was put in place and within a couple weeks, Sarah started to gain much needed weight. This story turned out well.

STORY: ATTORNEY ABUSE

In another case, an estate attorney was managing a large estate for a very elderly woman who had no heirs. She was leaving her estate to her favorite local charity. Some time went by after her death. At a fundraiser for this charity, one of her elderly friends went up to the treasurer of the organization and told him how happy the charity must be to get so much money from her deceased friend. The treasurer said he knew of no such person or their money, but he would definitely look into it. He did look into it and found that the attorney had simply taken the estate money for himself, thinking no one would know, as there were no family heirs. Had the casual conversation at the party not occurred, this woman's final wishes might never have come true.

STORY: ABUSE FROM WITHIN THE FAMILY

Sometimes the abuse comes from a family member who appears to be a loving caregiver. In one such case, the daughter was the sole caregiver of a demented mother. The daughter had called for help because, "I am at the end of my rope." The daughter had been the sole caregiver for almost a year without a break.

On doing the assessment, I noticed various staged bruises over several planes of the patient's body. When I asked the daughter about these, she shrugged them off stating the patient had either fallen or bumped into things. My impression was the daughter was a caring caregiver, but the bruises were troublesome. As a mandated reporter, I reported the case to APS.

After the APS caseworker had assessed the case, it turned out that the exhausted daughter had at times been rough with her mother especially when the mother tended to wander at night through the house.

Her mother's Alzheimer's symptoms were some of the hardest to manage, as she was like the Eveready bunny who slept in brief snatches and was on the move 24/7 displaying combative behavior, especially at night.

In this particular case, elder care management, agency caregivers, and APS formed a partnership of interventions for this daughter in getting her the respite and skills she needed as a caregiver. We placed agency caregivers in the home at night so the daughter could sleep. The money for the nighttime caregivers came from long distance adult children who really had no clue as to what had been happening.

After conducting a conference call with these adult children, they all chipped in a monthly monetary amount in order to give the caregiving daughter some assistance. Again this case turned out well with the daughter getting some breaks and enough sleep. We also connected her with a support group at the local Alzheimer's Association, which gave her the support and skills she desperately needed to continue as a caregiver for a demented adult.

Eventually, we got the mother into an adult day care two days a week (sliding fee), which gave the daughter time to begin to pick up the pieces of her life she had left behind. I continued to follow this case for months to be sure the interventions were working and allowing the daughter to be a compassionate caregiver to her mother.

TYPES OF ELDER ABUSE

Elder abuse is an umbrella term under which all acts of purposeful commission or omission are included in caring for an elder. All abuse, regardless of the type, causes undue stress, pain, anguish, injury, and loss of quality of life. What are some of the signs of elder abuse and what do you do if you suspect or witness elder abuse?

There are various types of elder abuse and each has its own signs.

Physical abuse. Causing physical injury and pain to an elder by hitting, slapping, restraining by physical or chemical means, and bruising by rough handling.

Sexual abuse. Any kind of non-consensual sexual contact with an elder.

Neglect. Failure of caregivers to provide the basics of care such as hydration, food, shelter, personal care, and medical care for the elder. This also includes self-neglect on the part of elders who can no longer care for themselves.

Emotional/psychological abuse. Verbal or non-verbal acts that humiliate, denigrate, or intimidate the elder. (Family members commit ninety percent of psychological abuse.)

Financial abuse/scam. Taking advantage of an elder by taking or misusing funds, property, or assets. Frail or demented elders are especially vulnerable.

Abandonment of an elder. Leaving alone a vulnerable elder who is no longer able to care for themselves or is at danger when left by themselves.[7]

RECOGNIZING ABUSE

The following signs may indicate some form of abuse:

■ Bruises, broken bones, broken glasses, burns indicating physical abuse.

■ An unexplained change in personality, withdrawal from people and interests, depression indicating emotional abuse. Witnessing verbal threats, denigration, or humiliations indicate verbal abuse.

■ Bruises around genitalia or breasts indicating sexual abuse.

■ Changes in bank accounts, large withdrawals of money, unrelated people moving in with the elder, newly executed documents, indicating financial abuse.

■ Weight loss, poor hygiene, pressure sores, lacking medical care indicate neglect.

■ Relationship issues between the elder and caregivers including family members may indicate abuse.[8]

WHAT DO YOU DO IF YOU SUSPECT ABUSE?

Be alert to changes in an elder's demeanor or personality or any other changes. Listen carefully to the elder. You do not have to be certain about the abuse or prove it before reporting. You just need to have a reasonable belief that abuse may have occurred. You can make anonymous reports. There are a number of places to report your suspicions. If you believe that the elder is in imminent danger, call 911.

Other than emergent situations, the foremost agency to call is the local Adult Protective Service (APS) or contact them online at www.napsa-now.org. You can find the number of APS where the elder resides by contacting The Eldercare Locator web site or calling 1-800-677-1116. This number is not available 24/7, so you can also find the local APS number by going to the National Center on Elder Abuse web site (www.ncea.aoa.gov) where you will find a state resource section.

You may also report to the local law enforcement agency. They may in some circumstances refer you to APS.

If you suspect abuse in a nursing facility or long-term care facility, you can call the local ombudsman. This is a person who investigates and resolves any complaints occurring in a facility. This number is always posted in the facility, usually in the entrance lobby. If you do not see it, ask for it.

If you are an elder who is being abused, tell someone you trust, such as a trusted family member, your physician, or a friend. You can also call APS and self-report.

WHAT CAN YOU EXPECT IF YOU CALL FOR HELP

You will be asked for information. Be prepared to give the name, address, and contact information of the elder. You will be asked what the concern is or why you are calling. You may be asked to give more specific information to corroborate your story such as the elder's care situation, family support, and any suspicious activity to warrant a belief that abuse is occurring such as yelling, or other abusive behavior. You may be requested to give your own information, but you can make the report anonymous if you wish.

WHAT ACTION IS TAKEN AFTER REPORTING?

APS will prioritize the report regarding its seriousness. You may not see action immediately. A caseworker is assigned to the case and investigates to see if abuse has occurred. If abuse has occurred, a plan is initiated to remedy the abuse, which may include referral to other community services. Some people including professional health providers, who have had experience with APS, believe that their reports did not make a difference. From my experience over the years, I have learned not to worry about this. If you believe abuse is continuing, make another report and another and another. If the same person or multiple people make reports on an elder, the priority or urgency increases, thus ensuring action.

PROTECTING AGAINST ELDER ABUSE

Enlist professional help. If necessary, get your financial and legal documents in order. Appoint a trusted person to either manage or oversee your finances.

Avoid becoming isolated. Maintain your social network.

Speak up. If unhappy with your care or you are feeling abused, tell a trusted person in your life.

Be skeptical. If it seems too good to be true, it probably is.

Protect your identity. Never provide any confidential information like your social security number or bank account number to anyone for any reason either by phone or online. People who need this information will not ask you to provide it by phone or online.

Say no! Do not be pressured by anyone to do something or buy something.

Some elders' conditions or history may make them more of a target for abuse. Such conditions are as follows:

- The growing intensity of an elder's dementia such as combativeness, which may try the caregiver's patience.

- Isolation where the caregiver and the elder are together constantly without support or respite.

- The elder may have been an abusive parent or spouse. These cases are particularly challenging, as the spouse or family caregiver may finally feel they are getting revenge for past hurts and abuses.

- A history of domestic violence in the home.

- The elder's own tendency toward verbal or physical aggression, which may increase with dementia. It is always an enormous challenge, as an elder care manager, to keep paid caregivers in a home where the elder is verbally nasty and/or physically or sexually aggressive. It takes all the professional skill from the physician, neurologist, counselors, care manager, and caregivers to resolve some of these issues. Caregivers also need to have a place of work that is safe and free from verbal, physical, and sexual harassment.

- Substance abuse including alcohol abuse. Substance abuse is the most frequent symptom involved with elder abuse and neglect. This involves not only the elder but also the caregivers.[9]

SCAMS

Scams involve ways to con an elder out of money or resources, or to obtain housing or other services from the elder.

STORY: MARRIAGE SCAM

 As a care manager, I was filling a mediplanner every two weeks for a very wealthy, elderly, demented woman who had agency caregivers around the clock. She had no living family. She usually made very little sense verbally, talking about things in the distant past, but that morning, as I carefully poured her meds into her planner, my red flags began to fly. She said, "I am getting married this afternoon." At first I just listened and made no comment, but she kept at it and seemed convinced that she was really getting married in just a couple of hours, even asking me what she should wear.

I finally stopped pouring her meds, sat down in front of her, and started to ask questions. I asked whom she was marrying. She replied, "Marcus, my caregiver." This was a paid male caregiver who slept overnight in her home in case she needed anything during the night, which was rare. When I asked who was going to perform the ceremony, she named a minister that I knew in the area. Although I kept telling myself this was probably all in her demented mind, the details were too specific. I finished the mediplanner and went back to the office.

I called the caregiver to come into the office immediately and then called the minister. Yes, he had an appointment to go to the home to perform a ceremony. When the caregiver was confronted in the office, he finally broke down and admitted to proposing. His reason was this. "I have lived in poverty all my life and this was my one chance to be rich!" This situation illustrates one reason to choose an agency that carefully monitors and checks the elder frequently to be sure the caregivers are following the care plan. This vigilance pays off in finding problems early.

Prime targets for scams are elders who live alone with no one watching or monitoring, an elder who craves socialization and is profoundly grateful for any attention, and elders with health issues.

The top ten scams targeting elders are as follows:

Medicare insurance fraud. People may pose as Medicare representatives to get personal information.

Counterfeit prescription drugs. This happens usually on the Internet where elders may shop for cheaper prescription medications.

Funeral & cemetery scams. These include unnecessary expenses charged by a funeral home, or con artists appearing at the funeral as announced in the obituaries to collect a fake debt from a grieving family.

Fraudulent anti-aging products.

Telemarketing. Elders are especially vulnerable; this age group makes twice as many purchases over the phone as the national average. There are three main examples:

- *The pigeon drop.* A scammer informs the elder they have won a large sum of money but in order to claim the prize, they have to pay a sum to cover some upfront costs.

- *The fake accident ploy.* A scammer tells the elder they must send money to a certain address to cover the costs of a family member who has had an accident or illness.

◄ *Charity scams.* Monies are solicited for a fake charity especially after a large natural disaster.

Internet fraud. This comes in all guises, but one of the most frequent is an email/phishing scam. These are emails that pose as a legitimate institution, such as a bank for example, and ask the elder for an update on their personal information.

Investment scams. Bernie Madoff comes to mind. This is another reason to have a certified professional trusted financial planner and/or elder law attorney helping to oversee an elder's monies.

Homeowner/reverse mortgage scams. Elders are especially vulnerable to these scams, as they target people who have paid off their homes. These scams try to tell elders to pay for an appraisal in order to lower their property taxes. Reverse mortgage scams can cause elders to lose their homes by offering "money" or a "free house" in exchange for their home.

Sweepstakes and lottery scams. This is a scam that requests a "fee" to claim their monetary prize. A legitimate lottery or sweepstakes will *never* ask for a fee! I, myself, have gotten several of these letters in the past year. Do not respond and shred the letter.

Grandparent scam. This is the most cost effective and the easiest scam. The elder is called, and the scammer pretends to be a grandchild who is in trouble and needs money immediately through Western Union or Moneygram. "Grandma, I am in the Tijuana jail and I need money to bail me out immediately!" [10]

PROTECTION FROM SCAMS

The National Consumers League's National Fraud Information Center has concise tips for avoiding these calls (www.fraud.org).[11]

- Sign up for the National Do Not Call Registry. You can do this either by phone or by computer. If calling by phone, it must be from the phone you want to register. The number is 1-888-382-1222. You can also register online at www.donotcall.gov. You will need Internet access and a working email address. A response will be sent to that email address with a link that must be clicked on within seventy-two hours to complete the registration. It may take up to thirty-one days for you to notice fewer calls.

- Registration expires in five years and you have to keep track as to when to renew.

- Some callers are not covered, like nonprofit groups, political organizations, and surveys.

- Some companies may still call if you have purchased an item or a service from them in the past. You can request that they remove you from their list.

- Be careful what you sign, as companies then have permission to call you. You can always request not to be called.

- You can enforce your rights if telemarketers ignore the fact that your number is on a do not call list. You can report them through the toll free number or web site.

- Educate mentally alert elders to NEVER give out financial information of any kind or to buy anything at the door, over the phone, or by mail without consulting with a trusted person. (Do NOT try to educate a demented elder. They are unable to learn or remember.)

■ There should be a trusted advisor (family member, attorney) involved with and regularly monitoring finances so they will notice when something is amiss.

■ When visiting an elder, be vigilant for telemarketing calls.

■ Monitor the mail and in some cases divert the mail.

STORY: MAIL SCAM

 Regular mail or snail mail, as opposed to email, is another matter. Sometimes mail that requests money is an even bigger problem. These requests, however, are not necessarily scams. I was care managing a beautiful elderly ninety-year-old woman with moderate short-term memory loss and other mild dementia symptoms. She lived alone and her long distance daughters were concerned that she was getting very forgetful and losing weight. She also could not manage her medication regime.

After many months of care management, I was at her modest apartment to monitor her weight and medications. She seemed agitated and just out of sorts. When I asked her what was wrong, she said, "It is the mail! I just do not know what to do with some of it." I was puzzled as we had set up a system to put all bills and other mail needing attention in a folder for the bill payer who came each month.

When asked to show me what mail was troubling her, she pulled out a letter with the local police logo on it requesting a donation for the upcoming policeman's ball. I said, "You do not have to pay this. This is just a request for a donation." She replied, "Oh yes I do. If I am in my car and the police stop me for any reason, they will know I did not donate and will not like me." (She still had her car, but depended on others to drive her places in her car.) It turns out she felt compelled to contribute to other requests for donations even though she did not have the resources to do so.

Although she was adamant about being independent and maintaining control over her checking account, we slowly convinced her to turn over her checkbook to the hired bill payer and to place *all* mail in the folder for the monthly bill payer to review. This was a hard battle, but she finally agreed.

Abuse and scams are not just about separate incidents that, once resolved, make everything fine. Abuse and scams change people, especially the elderly. It increases their fear, causing expenditure of energy to recoup losses, and makes them less trusting. It decreases their quality of life. It is the job of all of us interacting with elders to be educated and constantly vigilant to the ever-increasing problem of abuse and scams of the elderly.

TASK LIST

☐ IF POSSIBLE, EDUCATE THE ELDER ON HOW TO AVOID ELDER ABUSE AND SCAMS.

☐ ADVOCATES AND FAMILY MEMBERS NEED TO MONITOR THE ELDER FREQUENTLY FOR ANY SIGNS OF ABUSE OR SCAMS.

☐ PLACE THE ELDER ON A NATIONAL DO NOT CALL REGISTRY.

☐ IF CAREGIVERS ARE IN PLACE, MONITOR THE CAREGIVERS FREQUENTLY OR HIRE A CARE MANAGER TO MONITOR.

☐ KNOW YOUR LOCAL ADULT PROTECTIVE SERVICE NUMBER.

☐ LISTEN TO THE ELDER.

*"Life is not a journey to the grave with the
intention of arriving safely in a pretty and
well-preserved body. But rather, to skid in
broadside, thoroughly used up, totally worn out,
and loudly proclaiming.... WOW what a ride."*

■ MARK FROST [1]

CHAPTER TWELVE
DEATH AND GRIEF

In this Chapter…

■ FACING DEATH

■ UNDERSTANDING THE PROCESS OF DYING

■ PLANNING FOR DEATH AND DYING

■ STORIES OF DYING AND LESSONS LEARNED

■ DEALING WITH GRIEF

FACING DEATH

Could we please talk about the "D" word in our culture? Does the word, death, have to be such a scary taboo? In our freewheeling, young culture full of individualism and bravado plus leadership in technology and science, we have created a taboo around this event that *EVERYONE* will experience. When I first started to do hospice work, the scenario at times went something like this. Referred to a particular home to do a hospice admission, I am greeted at the door usually by a family member who immediately closes the door behind me. Before I can remove my coat, the family member puts a finger to their lips, and leads me to a dark corner of the house. "Do NOT mention the 'D' word or say the word, hospice!" they say. "He does not know." I try to ascertain just what the patient has been told by his or her physician and then proceed to the patient's room. I usually start out by introducing myself and asking the patient if he knows why I am there. This is the usual response. "Yes. I know why you are here. I am dying." So, there you go. All the secrecy and whispering that goes on around death and dying is really for naught, as even children have a sense when they are dying. I have often wondered in the wee hours of the morning why our culture has such fear and taboo around even mentioning the "D" word. We use any other word possible for death and dying. Here is a list mostly gleaned from obituaries, which I have read for decades:

◀ He passed or passed away.

◀ She left us on December 31st.

◀ He went to be with the Lord.

◀ She transitioned.

◀ He departed.

◀ She met her Maker on June 1st.

◀ He left this world in the fall of 1999.

◀ She rejoined her departed family.

◀ He left his earthly body and now has a heavenly body.

◀ She went to her eternal rest on January 12th.

I would never want to rob people of words that give them comfort, but sometimes the contortions we go through not to say the words "death, died, or dying," are counter-productive.

We have an unbelievable faith in science and technology to heal and cure anything. We are stunned when technology and science fail us. We spend great amounts of money on costly solutions that have poor outcomes and certainly do not contribute to any quality of life for either the patient or the family. We must talk with our loved ones about death and dying on a regular basis. We do not have to be obsessive about it or talk about it every day, just once in a while, especially as we begin the *Journey through Old*.

Felix Carrion, coordinator of the Stillspeaking Ministry of the United Church of Christ, recently wrote an online devotional essay on this topic.

When I turned fifty last month, my oldest son kidded with me. He said, "Well, Dad, it's downhill from here." We shared a hearty laugh. How does

one escape the sure lot that befalls everyone? How
do we reconcile ourselves with the ever-present
end? Moving onward and upward, there are some
resolutions I would like to work on for myself (and
offer to others as possibilities).

Meditate more on death. Although this sounds
morbid, it really isn't. The more one's mortality
becomes one's daily bread, the deeper the inhalation
and the longer the exhalation. The distinction
between the present hour and the eternal one will
incite awakened laughter when the virtual veil
between the two becomes completely translucent.[2]

Here is what the Dalai Lama says about death: "It is
very important to constantly familiarize our thoughts
and emotions with the idea of death so that it does not
arrive as something completely unexpected. We need to
accept death as part of our lives. This kind of attitude is
much healthier than simply trying not to think or talk
about death."

Elizabeth Kubler-Ross says this about dying: "It's only
when we truly know and understand that we have a limited time on earth — and that we have no way of knowing when our time is up — that we will begin to live each
day to the fullest, as if it was the only one we had."[3]

Dr. Atul Gawande, MD, author of the book, *Being
Mortal*, questions how medicine and our technological
society rob us of facing our end-of-life passage:

Technological society has forgotten what scholars
call the "dying role" and its importance to people
as life approaches its end. People want to share

memories, pass on wisdoms and keepsakes, settle relationships, establish their legacies, make peace with God, and ensure that those who are left behind will be okay. They want to end their stories on their own terms. The role is, observers argue, among life's most important, for both the dying and those left behind. And if it is, the way we deny people this role, out of obtuseness and neglect, is cause for everlasting shame. Over and over, we in medicine inflict deep gouges at the end of people's lives and then stand oblivious to the harm done.[4]

TALKING ABOUT DEATH AND DYING

Talking about death and dying may bring tears initially. I remember well when I first broached the topic with my own aging mother and father. They both looked at me like deer caught in the headlights. My father said, "That is a topic not up for discussion!" His eyes filled with tears, and he was not a crying man. My mother took me aside later and warned me to never bring up the topic again. "It is upsetting to your Father." I would like to say that eventually they became more comfortable with the topic. I did bring it up again in the guise of wanting to follow their wishes as to an advanced directive, powers of attorneys for health and finance, funeral arrangements, obituaries, cremation vs. burial, location of important papers, etc. The only thing my Father would say is he did not want cremation. He wanted to be buried. He refused to reveal if he had a will or trust, or where any final written arrangements were kept. My parents even in their eighties were in denial of their own deaths and could not imagine dying. If one is in denial, one does not have to plan or even think about something. Like the prince, we can remain in our castles and pretend such a thing does not exist. Throughout this guide-book, you can see that this may cause bad things to happen, which are easily preventable.

Talking about death will eventually lessen the terror. Eventually we realize that we all die, so why not talk about it. Talking about a loved one's death or talking about how one spouse will get along without the other spouse helps to cushion future grief. Talking initiates planning so there is not such a crisis around the actual event. It is truly a loving and considerate thing for all concerned.

UNDERSTANDING THE PROCESS OF DYING

Elisabeth Kubler-Ross was a pioneer on the death and dying process plus she helped to found the hospice movement. Her research documented the five stages of grief when facing a terminal diagnosis and death: denial, anger, bargaining, depression, and acceptance. There is no special order to these and one does not necessarily move smoothly from one to the other, but generally all are present somewhere along the process.

Many patients and their families have often asked me just what does the dying process look like. The best resource I have found for this issue is a small booklet called *Gone From My Sight*, by Barbara Karnes, found on Amazon.com (or www.bkbooks.com).[5] This small book tells it like it is starting at one to three months prior to death. There is again no set formula as to how these events or stages occur. Each death is as individual as the person going through the process. There is no formula or specific words when talking to someone about dying. It is different for every individual and situation. The most important thing you can do is listen. Listen to what the person near death is saying. Give them time to respond. It may not be easy for them to respond immediately. Do not let your own discomfort with silence or waiting for a response intrude by saying platitudes that do not fit.

One of the most difficult stages for loved ones is the dying person's withdrawal usually one to three months before death. They may withdraw from former interests, from long-time friends, and even close family members. Going through the dying process with a very dear friend of mine, the hardest thing she asked me to do was call her circle of close, long-time friends and tell them she no longer wanted them to call or visit. Sleeping at this time may increase. Words may decrease, and touch and just being still with the dying person may be what is most needed. Eating and drinking also may decrease. Most families may accept that eating is decreasing but they have enormous difficulty with the decrease in fluids. As the body shuts down, the kidneys and lungs may not be able to handle fluids.

One to two weeks before death, the dying person may become disoriented and confused. There may be fluctuations in blood pressure, pulse, and body temperature. Skin color and breathing patterns may change, and signs of respiratory congestion may be present. Both bowel and bladder function may change.

One to two days before death, there may or may not be a rally, which leads family members to ask if the person is "getting better." All the above signs now increase in frequency and intensity until the dying person becomes unresponsive. Death occurs when the dying person stops breathing. It is the hospice staff's job to manage all of these symptoms, so the dying person is comfortable and as pain free as possible.

In this process, do not be afraid that the dying person may become addicted to pain medications. Hospice staff are skilled in pain management and want to maintain the most optimum pain free environment for the patient as possible. Patients may also fight pain medications, as they want to be alert and not sleepy with medication. Pain medications do cause sleepiness but usually only for a couple days until the body gets used to the pain medication and the new dosage.

It is thought that our hearing sense is the last sense to leave our bodies, and it may still be present even when breathing ceases. Speaking quietly to your loved one or playing soft music creates an atmosphere of peace and support for all concerned. It is suggested that you do this for fifteen to twenty minutes after breathing has stopped.

WHAT TO DO AFTER DEATH OCCURS

What do you actually do once your loved one dies or you think they may have died? There are basically two procedures to use, which depends if the patient is on hospice or not.

If at home on the hospice program, you will immediately call the hospice number and report the death. A nurse will come to your home as soon as she is able and confirm the death. The nurse will help and provide whatever support is needed, including calling the funeral home, notifying the physician, and arranging for removal of all medical equipment and medications.

If the loved one is not on hospice, you call 911. You *must* have the "do not resuscitate" order signed by the physician or a physician's order for life-sustaining treatment signed by the physician to hand to the emergency medical crew when they arrive. An advanced directive (not signed by a physician) is not applicable in this situation. If you do not have these documents, they may perform life saving measures, including CPR, and may transport the patient to the hospital.

After a significant loss, the funeral is over, and everyone has returned home, the remaining spouse or partner is now truly alone — sometimes for the first time in his life. The big house may no longer fit. This is when the rubber meets the road. Often friends do not stay in touch because, "I just do not know what to say or do." "When I try to visit with Fred, he cries. I just do not want to go see him." Not only do people not know what to do or say, but also this kind of grief reminds them of what may happen to them in the future, and they do not want to think about it. And yet we all know that this denial robs us not only of our humanity and compassion but also robs us of the opportunity to be better prepared for our own losses in the future. If we live long enough, we are going to suffer losses. There is no way to get around this.

In some circumstances, in spite of our best efforts to be present with someone suffering decline due to loss or other reasons, that individual rebuffs us. She may slam the door in your face or may not pick up the phone when called. He will get into a spiral of grief, depression, decline, or isolation, and will refuse any socialization or assistance. I have intimate experience with this spiral, as this is what happened to my mother after the loss of her spouse.

STORY: DEALING WITH THE LOSS OF A SPOUSE

When counselors, psychiatrists, and medications failed to bring my mother out of her prolonged grief and depression, my brother and I were told to take her to live near us. We found a retirement facility near both of us and tried to set up her apartment exactly as her former home had been. During her first week in her new home, she actually made a new friend, and the two of them participated in many activities offered by the facility. We were all enthused and hopeful. My brother and I continued to be very attentive taking her on outings on a regular basis. I thought we had really turned a corner, but after about two months, her friend was diagnosed with terminal cancer and died quickly in a matter of weeks. This was devastating for my mother who by this time was also losing her sight due to macular degeneration, the leading cause of blindness in the elderly.

By now, I was overwhelmed by the amount of time and effort it was taking to care for my mother, and yet the situation did not seem to be improving in spite of our best efforts. We had everything in place. My brother and I were her advocates, all paperwork was completed and in order, we had established her with a primary care physician and specialists including a counselor, her medications were being administered as prescribed, she was in a safe environment, and we were making every effort to make sure she had as much socialization and stimulation possible to ensure a reasonable quality of life. Why wasn't it working? Where was the mother I had always known, loved, and wanted back?

One day after work, I dropped in on my minister who happened to still be in his office. I sat down and related all that had happened — my parent's sixty-year marriage, my father's sudden death, and my mother's decline. He listened without interrupting for a long time. He then said something to me, which helped me cope for the next few years until my mother died. It went something like this: "You and your brother have done everything humanly possible for your mother. It does not matter whether the marriage was good or bad; sixty years of marriage is a long time, and your mother may never be herself again after such a loss. At this point, your job is to love your mother as she is now in this present condition and do not necessarily expect her to change."

Suddenly a weight seemed lifted from my shoulders. Sometimes, in spite of putting all the pieces in place and bringing love and compassion to a situation, it does not work out like *you* want it to. On the plus side, my mother had her physical health in that she had no major illnesses or conditions other than a vision deficit, and she was in a safe and beautiful environment near people who loved her. She was living her life the best she could under the circumstances and for the most part making her own decisions. I let go of the mother I used to have and started to embrace the mother I presently had. This may not sound like a big deal, but for me, it was huge. It enabled me to stop worrying and fretting, expecting her to get better and allowed me to start observing my mother in a new light. I had a new lightness around her, and a sense of humor developed between the two of us. I started to see my mother laugh, rarely, but it was a start. I believe that accepting and affirming my mother as she was at that time set us both free.

I wish I could say that this story had a happy ending and that my mother continued to improve, but that was not the case. My mother continued to struggle with her loneliness and depression without my father until the end of her life. My brother and I plus her grandchildren, daughter-in-law, and friends continued to bring her solace.

PLANNING FOR DEATH AND DYING

So what are the things to talk about and plan around death and dying?

Talk about the easiest things first. Many people are able to make arrangements for their final resting place ahead of time. The choices are not many or difficult. You can either be buried, cremated, contribute your body to science, or a fourth option, called a green burial has surfaced in the past ten years. When you have made a decision, *write it down and let your family know where it is.*

> ***Burial.*** This method may or may not include embalming with fluids to preserve the body especially if there is going to be a viewing plus some sort of coffin or casket. My mother, stunned at the sudden death of her eighty-six-year-old husband, was overwhelmed with the choices of coffins and caskets. She finally picked out the top of the line, which was thousands of dollars she did not have. As her advocate, I gently steered her away from this choice towards another she could afford. All we knew of Dad's wishes was where he wanted to be buried, and he had bought a gravesite. We had a simple memorial service and a brief graveside service all managed by

the funeral home, which we called in the middle of the night after he died. Since there was no planning, there were a myriad of decisions to be made quickly. My mother was overwhelmed, so my brother and I did the best we could. When working with families, I try to get them to make some of these decisions ahead of time.

Cremation. This is the act of burning the body at high temperatures reducing the body to ash and bone fragments. It was the choice my mother made. Like my father, it was the one thing she made arrangements for ahead of time. This time, I was determined to be better organized than we were with my father. I asked my minister for community resources regarding cremations. I lined up the funeral home that performed cremations, and gave them all the information about my mother. When the time came, all paperwork and plans were in place. I was glad she chose this method, as I wanted to keep a part of her with me. I let the funeral home know this, and they provided me with a small urn, which I keep in a special place in my home. The rest of the remains were shipped to a burial site next to my father.

Donating bodies to science (also called willed body programs). If you want to donate your body to science, do an online search for *willed body program* and click on your state or your alma mater/university where medical schools are located. The procedure varies from state to state. If you want to donate body parts or organs, you must indicate this on your driver's license.

Green Alternatives. A definition of this option is from Barbara Kate Repa from www.caring.com.

> A green funeral involves conducting final arrangements and disposing of a body in ways that restore and conserve the environment, without using the harmful chemicals and non-biodegradable materials commonly used by the funeral industry. This means no embalming, no burial vaults (concrete or metal vaults), and choosing only more modern cremation facilities technologically engineered to lessen the carbon footprint. If you want any remains to be buried, there are green burial grounds that adhere to practices that restore or conserve plants, landscapes, and native materials, and use no pesticides in maintaining the grounds. They limit the types, sizes, and visibility of grave markers to preserve natural vistas.[6]

These options are especially important to people who have lived intentionally on the earth and want to leave the smallest footprint possible.

ENGAGING HOSPICE

The hospice movement is now well established in our culture as an option for elders since Medicare resources now fund it. Hospice is another topic to talk about before it may be needed. Not everyone wants to avail themselves of this option because you have to accept the fact that you are dying and give up active or curative treatment for your terminal disease. Hospice provides palliative care, which manages symptoms and pain. The dying person is kept comfortable, with pain and other symptoms managed by a caring team of professionals made up of a physician, registered nurses, social workers, home health aides for personal care, a chaplain, counselors, and volunteers. A physical therapist may be used for safety concerns and equipment issues. Bereavement services are offered to the family after death occurs. This may include individual or group counseling led by trained grief therapists.

You are referred to hospice after you, your family, and your physician decide that curative treatments are no longer effective. A physician order is necessary. This service can be given in the patient's home, but it is also available in facilities as skilled nursing homes, adult family homes, hospitals, free standing hospices, and assisted living facilities. The great majority of hospice services are given in the patient's home. In the home setting, the hospice patient does not have, except in very unusual circumstances, 24/7 care, nor are hospice staff necessarily present at the moment of death. I have had patients tell me on admission to hospice home care, "Well what good is that! I need 24/7 care and I do not want to be alone when the death of my loved one occurs." The hospice team works intensively with families and patients to alleviate these fears and find solutions.

ENGAGING THE ELDER'S PHYSICIAN

It is also not necessary to go on hospice. You may want to continue treatment or you simply may want your physician to provide the support and symptom management.

Speaking with your spouse or other family members about death may prove the hardest part of all. It is unbearable for some people to think about life without their soul mate of many years. The emotions, fears, and tears that this conversation might engender are too much, but for those who accomplish this difficult task, the way forward is much easier after one of them has died. Some topics needing discussion are possible changes in living venues, financial issues for the remaining spouse, location of important papers or documents, wishes for funeral and memorial service, obituaries, arrangements for cherished pets, etc.

PREPARING FOR LOSS

One couple actually sat down and courageously wrote down each of their roles. She had always cooked. He had never cooked. He had always paid the bills. She barely knew how to write a check. He had always maintained the outside and she had always maintained the inside. He always took care of and maintained the cars. She had no clue as to car care.

After all their respective tasks had been written down, they switched roles. He did all of her tasks, and she did all of his. She showed him how to make menus for the week, draw up a shopping list, buy and put away food, and prepare the meal. She laughingly told me, "At first, meals were a little rough." He taught her how to pay bills, reconcile a checking account, and how to keep tax records. They decided and gave permission to each other to hire out some of these tasks when one of them died. Yard and car maintenance were two of these items. Over months, they slowly taught each other to do each of their respective tasks. They promised each other not to neglect their interests if one of them died.

He was an avid golf player and she loved to sew and cook. They even gave each other permission to find love again and marry. When she died of cancer, he grieved, but remembered all they had discussed. He was grateful they had done this and found his grief much more bearable. He continued his golf game as promised, and several years later, he remarried. The amazing thing that happened in this process was the naturalness and humor that these two people slowly developed over their own demise.

STORIES OF DYING AND LESSONS LEARNED

Here are some examples of some death scenarios that I have experienced through the decades of doing this work. Some may speak to you or not. Some of these experiences happened years ago and others are relatively recent. They remain in my memory as if they happened yesterday. They each have a title reflecting the lesson learned.

DAMAGING WORDS

 This involves the death of a child. Many years ago I worked in a children's hospital on a floor for newborns to two years. One evening a child I had nursed for many weeks was dying. The young mother was quietly sobbing by her child's crib. On the other side of the room, a mother and father were praying loudly and fervently for their child's recovery with many members of their faith community surrounding the crib and singing. The other mother and father came over to the young mother and said their child was improving because God had heard their prayer and the prayers of hundreds who were on their prayer chain.

I heard this exchange and watched as the single mother sank to the floor. I know the other parents of the recovering child did not mean harm, but these were damaging words to the single mother. A cold fury arose in my gut. I went and put my arms around her. She said softly through her sobs, "Did I not pray enough or have enough people pray for my child?" Holding her, I said, "God did not will your child to suffer and die. Your prayers mattered, and it does not make a difference how many people pray for something. One person's prayer is all that is needed. God's arms are around you now." No words are better than damaging words.

WORDS OF SOLACE

 An elderly couple had been devoted to each other for over fifty years when the wife was hospitalized for a sudden acute illness and died. The husband was inconsolable. Those of us on duty left him with some private time with his wife, but heaving with sobs, he continued to cling to her body.

I called the hospital chaplain even though it was the middle of the night. The chaplain walked quietly into the room and put his hands on the man's shoulders. He bent down and whispered into the man's ear, "She is not here, but you will see her again. In the meantime, she lives in your heart and you can call on her at any time." The husband slowly reacted to these words. He stood up, squared his shoulders and walked from the room. His grieving was by no means over, but something in those caring words delivered in a calm and comforting manner spoke to him.

NO WORDS NEEDED

 This event occurred in Africa where I spent over two years in a remote hospital. A young woman was brought into the hospital with a rare terminal disease. The family dropped her off and returned to their village. Because she spoke a dialect that none of the African staff knew, communication was practically nil. Her small private hospital room was stark. She would lie quietly for hours just staring at the ceiling.

I visited her several times a day sitting silently and holding her hand. I brought a fresh flower each morning and evening for her to look at, so she did not have to just stare at the bare walls and ceiling. She rarely looked at me but did not resist my holding her hand. I was holding her hand when death seemed near. Suddenly she gripped my hand, brought it to her mouth, and kissed it. She slowly closed her eyes and died.

At that moment, there was an experience I had never had before. I was aware of her spirit, which seemed to fill that small room to the bursting point. It was palpable. It was as if the very air was thick, and then it was gone like a strong wind had just left the room. It was as if the room could simply no longer hold her spirit. I have never forgotten this young woman who touched me in such a profound way.

A RARE FAMILY

A father had gone onto hospice with terminal cancer when the family called for care management. The mother was also terminally ill but not as close to death as the father. The care needs of both parents were overwhelming, even to me, and I knew this would be one of the more complicated cases I had ever managed. Both parents wanted to remain in their home to die.

This was a large family with five adult children who began to come from various parts of the country to be with their parents in their last days. Having dealt with large families in the past, I somewhat dreaded these arrivals as more often than not, adult children may not agree on how the last days should play out. There may be old rivalries that arise and old resentments that get in the way of a peaceful time. This family was different. Not only did they all get along with each other, but they had a deep respect and profound love for their parents. They divided up the tasks among themselves without complaint. Plans had been put in place, paperwork was in order, and both the parents and adult children spent quality time talking and laughing with each other.

I actually enjoyed going there, as there was always something wonderful coming out of the oven, conversation and laughter were everywhere even with the all-consuming care needs of these two beloved, dying people. There was lightness in this home in spite of what was happening. The agency caregivers also enjoyed working in this home. Usually when care needs are this heavy with two patients instead of just one, we burn through caregivers rather quickly. The work is simply too labor intensive. These caregivers did not want to leave because the entire family was deeply grateful for the caregivers and expressed this appreciation openly and often. That can make all the difference for those on the front lines of care.

One afternoon as I was working for this family alongside the hospice nurse filling mediplanners, I went to the bedroom to see how the father was doing. He was lying in bed and asked if I would help him get up for just a few minutes. I slowly transferred him to a bedside chair where he sat exhausted from the exertion. He slumped forward in a brief moment of despair. He had been a strong and successful man. "This thing has really got me, hasn't it?" he said. Kneeling down in front of him, I lifted his head and said, "It may have gotten your physical body, but the strength and wisdom you have passed to your children is phenomenal and will continue to live and grow." He stayed in the chair only a couple more minutes and then requested to go back to bed. It was the last time he was able to sit up. He died a few days later.

When visiting the family a few days after the death, they were all in the living room planning a memorial service in their back yard. Even though their mother was not able to communicate due to dementia, they were fully including her in the planning.

When I asked the son about their plans, he said, "We are going to get Mom squared away first. She will go live near one of my siblings. Once that is done we will all deal with the house and its contents."

The priorities were clear, a plan had been made, and everyone was contributing. When the hospice nurse and I walked out of the house, I turned to her and asked if she had ever seen such a family so together and prepared. "Hardly ever. It is so rare," she replied.

It does not have to be rare! It could be far more common if we took the time to prepare and talk to each other about one of the most profound events in our lives — our own death.

A CHILD'S WISDOM

Serving as a school nurse at public grade schools, one of my tasks was to oversee the welfare of a nine-year-old boy named Steven. Steven was extremely frail due to a congenital heart defect and was on a waiting list for a heart-lung transplant. At the time, this was a highly experimental and risky procedure, but it was the only hope for Steven. If there was any flu or respiratory illness going around the school or excessive absenteeism due to a respiratory illness, Steven was to stay out of school until the episode had passed.

One day, as I reviewed the absentee records, it became clear that it would be in Steven's best interests to leave school for a few days. I went to his class and signaled for him to leave his classroom. We sat in the hallway as I explained why it was best that he go home.

He looked at me with his huge eyes in his pale, thin face and said, "I can't go home now! It is math time, and I love math!"

"OK," I said, "how about right after math."

"No!" he said. "That is history time and I love history!"

"OK, then as soon as history is over, I will take you home."

"NO!" he almost wailed.

"Why not?" I asked, with a hint of exasperation entering my voice.

"Because that is recess! It is the most important part of the day! It is when we play!"

One cannot argue with the wisdom of a nine-year-old. I wish I could say that Steven received his heart-lung transplant and went on to live a long and productive life, but that would not be real. Steven died a few months later quietly in his sleep, but the profoundly wise words of a little boy will always remain in my heart. Steven on several occasions had talked to me about the fact that he may be dying. Leaning his frail body against mine as we sat on my office couch, he spoke about his dreams for his future but then got quiet saying those dreams might not have time to come true. In spite of his precarious condition, Steven had his priorities in order. He cherished every moment of every day and he also knew that play was the most important part of the day.

DEALING WITH GRIEF

Now that hopefully the essential elements of the plan are in place and you have begun the conversations with your loved ones about death and dying, let's look at grief.

What is it? How long does it last? What can one do to get through a grief process? How does one support others going through a grief process?

According to just one definition on www.helpguide. org, "grief is a natural response to loss. It's the emotional suffering you feel when something or someone you love is taken away."[7] Listen to another definition by Kate Maloy in her book, *Every Last Cuckoo*, when the main character, Sarah loses her devoted husband, Charles.

> Sarah was sometimes ruled by stark pain, lost to everything else. Grief slipped away, only to attack from behind. It changed shape endlessly. It lacerated her, numbed her, stalked her, startled her, caught her by the throat. It deceived her eye with glimpses of Charles, her ear with the sound of his voice. She would turn and turn, expecting him, and find him gone. Again. Each time Sarah escaped her sorrow, forgetful amid other things, she lost him anew the instant she remembered he was gone.[8]

I do not think I have ever read a more powerful expression of just what grief is.

As we mentioned previously, Elisabeth Kubler-Ross mapped out the five stages of grief: denial, anger, bargaining, depression, and acceptance. As part of these stages, there may also be deep sadness, physical pain, sleep deprivation, stress, forgetfulness, anxiety, fear, guilt, and in some cases relief. Grief is unique to each person and there is no set formula as to how to grieve just as there is not a timeline when grief is over. Time does heal in its own way, but you are changed forever by grief. I have heard people say eventually grief is like the scar on a deep wound. You can always feel the scar, which feels different from the rest of your body. Some sources say that grief takes at least two years to go through, but for others, it takes much longer. Eventually, we may get to the point as quoted by author, George Eliot. "She was no longer wrestling with her grief, but could sit down with it as a lasting companion and make it a sharer in her thoughts."[9]

Grieving is part of being human, and we have all grieved. At a grief workshop I recently attended, we were all asked to write down times of grief. The list was lengthy from losing a loved one to losing a job, the death of a pet, being denied acceptance to a college of your dreams, having your house burglarized, losing your home to fire, having a miscarriage, divorce, losing a favorite tree to weather, infertility, loss of a lifelong dream, and loss of health. These were all listed as reasons to grieve.

Dr. William Solan, medical director for Geropsychiatric Center at Northwest Hospital, Seattle, asks:

> But what if time doesn't heal all wounds? How do you know when sad is just too sad? Sometimes extended periods of grief can lead to depression. The longer seniors mourn, the more at risk for depression they become. Depression resulting from grief is a biological manifestation like diabetes or cancer. As much as those two physical illnesses need treatment, so do mental ones like grief and depression.[10]

This is when normal grief that most people have when experiencing loss, becomes complicated grief which is debilitating and prolonged. This type of grief often requires professional intervention in both inpatient and outpatient settings.

What can one do to care for oneself during this time? Again there is no tried and true formula. Slow down. Take your time to get through this process, which cannot be hurried. Maintaining your social network, eating, getting enough sleep, exercising are all tips to remember as one goes through a grief process. At the grief workshop mentioned earlier, we received a handout entitled "Self Care During the Grieving Process." It divided the self-care into four areas: Physical, spiritual, intellectual, and social/emotional.

PHYSICAL

◀ Get regular exercise, including yoga or other meditative disciplines.

◀ Rest. Take naps.

◀ Eat healthy foods.

◀ Limit use of alcohol and drugs.

◀ Pamper yourself. Get a massage.

◀ Slow down.

SPIRITUAL

◀ Meditate or pray.

◀ Attend a spiritual retreat.

◀ Read spiritual wisdom.

◀ Work with a spiritual mentor.

◀ Create rituals.

◀ Be in nature.

◀ Journal your feelings.

◀ Look for daily miracles.

INTELLECTUAL

◀ Learn something new.

◀ Read helpful books that give you perspective.

SOCIAL/EMOTIONAL

◀ Work with a therapist.

◀ Join a support group.

◀ Connect with trusted friends.

◀ Participate in a faith community.[11]

Complicated grief is where the grief becomes so unbearably acute over a long period of time that it prohibits the grieving person from moving forward and accepting the loss. It is what happened to my mother. She refused to eat. She lost thirty pounds. She slammed the door in the face of long-time friends and became isolated. She rejected all offers of help and solace. She was angry and bitter that her spouse had abandoned her. She lost all sense of self-esteem. She literally could not function. This serious condition will require the help of a professional grief counselor or therapist. Do not wait to get this help as prolonged complicated grief has serious consequences both physically and mentally.

How can family members and friends support a grieving person? Being there for a grieving person can be one of life's most satisfying experiences and yet many people pull away at this time. They state they do not know what to do or what to say. It is simply too uncomfortable for them for many reasons. Responding to a grieving person who has just lost a loved one or being with someone who is dying will bring up your own issues around death and dying, including losing someone you may love. Many of us are doers, and we take action to solve problems. In this experience, taking action or knowing what to say is not necessarily required. Just being there and listening are all that is necessary. Here are some things from my own experience and from information read over the decades that may help you help someone else going through the dying and grieving process.

> **_Listen._** Do not judge their emotions or experience. Be still. Do not try to fill the silence. Use the "D" word. "I am so sorry your husband died…" This may give permission to the grieving person to actually feel more comfortable to talk with you about what they are going through and how their loved one died. Hold their hand or hug them if it seems appropriate. Try to avoid excessive chatter to fill the silence. According to the American Hospice Foundation, avoid the following comments: "I know how you feel." "It's part of God's plan." "Look what you have to be thankful for." "He's in a better place now." "This is behind you now; it's time to get on with your life." "You should" or "You will." Here is one I have heard on several occasions, "God never sends us more than we can bear."[12] These comments are not helpful.

Offering specific assistance. I have often heard people tell a dying or grieving person, "Call me if you need help." People are very reluctant to do that due to all the reasons we have already discussed. Offer specific assistance such as, "I will bring dinner over tomorrow," or "I will be over on Tuesday to do the laundry and change the bed for you," or "Make a grocery list; I am going to the store this afternoon and will get whatever is on your list." This is just not a one-time offer. Be consistent and keep circling back to observe what is needed and then offer. Other offers may include picking up children, transportation, walks, housework, bill assistance, pet care, sharing an enjoyable activity.

Provide ongoing support. Once the initial shock of the death and funeral is over and everyone has returned to his or her own life, the real work and process of grieving begins. The home seems empty and loneliness closes in. This is the time to stay in touch. Drop by, bring a meal, send a card, phone just to talk, offer an outing, etc.

Awareness. Be sensitive and attentive around holidays and other times that may be difficult for the grieving person. Offer some companionship at these times.

Do not expect that you will be able to do all of these things listed. Choose one or two and do those consistently which lets the person and/or family know they can count on you.

What follows now are some words written by others as they have traversed this journey of grief and dying.

Henry Van Dyke wrote the following words found in the pamphlet, "Gone From My Sight," by Barbara Karnes:

I am standing upon the seashore. A ship at my side spreads her white sails to the morning breeze and starts for the blue ocean. She is an object of beauty and strength. I stand and watch her until at length she hangs like a speck of white cloud just where the sea and sky come to mingle with each other.

Then someone at my side says: "There, she is gone!" "Gone where?"

Gone from my sight. That is all. She is just as large in mast and hull and spar as she was when she left my side and she is just as able to bear her load of living freight to her destined port.

Her diminished size is in me, not in her. And just at the moment when someone at my side says: "There, she is gone!" there are other eyes watching her coming, and other voices ready to take up the glad shout: "Here she comes!" And that is dying.

These are words from Henry Scott Holland.[13]

Remember, death is nothing at all. It does not count. I have only slipped away into the next room. Nothing has happened. Everything remains exactly as it was. I am I and you are you, and the old life that we lived so fondly together is untouched, unchanged. Call me by the familiar name. Speak of me in the easy way, which you always used. Put no difference in your tone. Wear no forced air of solemnity or sorrow. Laugh, as we always laughed, at the little jokes that we enjoyed together. Play, smile, think of me, pray for me. Let my name be ever the household word that it always was. Let it be spoken without an effort, without the ghost of a shadow upon it. Life means all that it ever meant. It is the same as it ever was. There is absolute and unbroken continuity. What is this death but a negligent accident? Why should I be out of mind because I am out of sight? I am but waiting for you, for an interval — somewhere very near, just around the corner. All is well.

TASK LIST

☐ HAVE ALL DOCUMENTATION UP TO DATE AND IN A PLACE WHERE FAMILY OR ADVOCATES CAN FIND THEM.

☐ TALK ABOUT DEATH AND YOUR END-OF-LIFE WISHES WITH LOVED ONES, PHYSICIANS, AND YOUR ELDER LAW ATTORNEY.

☐ MAKE PLANS FOR LOVED ONES LEFT BEHIND AFTER YOUR DEATH. THIS INCLUDES FUNERAL PLANS, FINANCIAL PLANS, RESIDENCE ISSUES, TAX ISSUES, BILL PAYING, HOME MANAGEMENT, CAR MANAGEMENT, AND LEGAL CHANGES.

☐ MEDITATE ON DEATH. IT CAN REMOVE THE FEAR AND EASES GRIEF.

☐ LEARN MORE ABOUT GRIEF AND WHAT IT TAKES TO GET THROUGH THIS TRANSITION.

EPILOGUE

New science and technology will vastly impact our aging in the future. Our children and grandchildren will age in very different ways than our parents aged and we are aging. There is no doubt that we will live increasingly longer lives due to this new science and technology, and we will be living our lives with better quality and with less chronic disease. TED talk futurist, Ray Kurzweil, and biogerontologist, Aubrey de Grey, theorize that our lives can be extended without today's degenerative processes using the new science involved with genes, nutrition, lifestyle changes, and medical advances that will be a part of our lives by 2020. Cynthia Kenyon, biochemist, has also done groundbreaking work that hints of longer, high quality lives absent of aged related diseases and conditions.

Laura Carstensen, psychologist and founder/director of the Stanford Center on Longevity, states that in 2015, there will be more people in the United States over the age of fifty than under the age of fifteen years old. We have gone from a pyramid shape of population with a large base of young people and few aged people at the top to a rectangle shaped population, as science and technology continue to solve some of the issues with aging. What does that mean for us as a culture? Terms like *old age* will transition to *long-lived*. Terms like "retirement" will take on new meaning with many long-lived elders working well into their elder years. Some elders may begin whole new careers in their later lives. The wisdom and knowledge that elders possess will have new value and will be appreciated for the richness this brings to our culture.

Degenerative diseases like Alzheimer's disease, arthritis with joint degeneration, other forms of dementia, diabetes, chronic respiratory diseases, and heart disease may all decline due to the new advances. As good as this all sounds, it is still in the future. There are many things that you can do right now, however, that may prolong your life and enable you to live a high quality of life not seen in previous generations.

Dan Buettner, *National Geographic* writer and explorer of the world's longest-lived peoples, has explored what are known as Blue Zones.[1] These are areas of the world where people live in good health into their hundreds. He states that nine percent of our chance at longevity is due to our genes. The other ninety-one percent is due to lifestyle. That is the good news because that is something we can all do something about! Although centenarians (those reaching one hundred years or older) are the fastest growing segment of the population, in reality only about one in five thousand reach that age.

One of the Blue Zones in is the highlands of Sardinia, a large island off the west coast of Italy. This is a culture where wisdom and age are honored and celebrated. They eat a plant-based diet. Elders live in community and are tenderly cared for. Due to their mountainous terrain, they walk daily over arduous trails getting exercise every day. They continue to farm, tend flocks, chop wood and live as they have always lived in relatively good health and without diminution.

Another Blue Zone is on the Japanese Island of Okinawa. These people not only live a long life but also die rather quickly rather than in a chronic disease state. They also have a plant-based diet and many grow their own food not only for themselves but to share with others. They have a tight friendship group, which lasts their whole lives. They have no word for retirement but continue to live out their passions right up to their deaths. They stay active either gardening, walking, spending time with their friendship group, and take great joy in the village children and their grandchildren. Isolation kills, and this culture has figured out how to stay connected and involved.

When these Blue Zones are looked at collectively, we find commonalities similar to the Centenarian Longevity Study mentioned earlier. They move naturally as they always have. They don't "exercise" as we have learned, but they keep moving with walking and gardening. Their whole lives are lives of movement. They take time for spirituality and develop a sense of purpose in their lives. They take time for downtime. They eat wisely, eating mostly plants in small amounts. Their alcohol use is small. They cherish connectedness and maintain the same friendships throughout their lives, or in other words, "someone always has their back." They are closely connected to their families. They do not divide their lives into *work lives* and *retirement lives* as we do in the United States. They continue to do work they enjoy all their lives.

Although some of these things are not possible for all of us, many of them are ideas that we can and should incorporate into our lives now. Eating a mostly plant-based regime, using reasonable portion control, moving everyday by walking or gardening, and maintaining an optimum weight would significantly decrease many of our chronic aging conditions and diseases. Maintaining a strong social network with friends and families and living in a community would keep us passionately alive and connected even through tough times. Seeing our aging as a time of potential instead of a pathological condition and a time to fear is a transition whose time has come. Get ready! The future is coming, and it looks good.

So, we come to the end of this guidebook. We have not covered everything, but if you can accomplish these tasks armed with whatever knowledge you have gleaned from these pages, you will have gone miles in making the *Journey through Old* easier and one of Grace.

Oh yes! I almost forgot. On this journey, do not forget to play. In Steven's words, "It is the most important part of each day!"

GLOSSARY

Activities of Daily Living (ADLs) – A list of daily self-care tasks used to evaluate the ability to live independently. These tasks include transferring (getting oneself from a lying to a sitting position and from a sitting to a standing position), walking, toileting oneself, bathing, dressing, and eating.

Adult Day Health Care (ADHC) – In addition to social activities, these centers offer health related services, physical therapy, occupational therapy, speech therapy, a nurse on duty, possibly a social worker, care management, and a physician available. Some offer disease management services for chronic conditions such as hypertension, diabetes, and cardiac conditions. Some are specialized for Alzheimer's care.

Advanced Directives – A category of legal documents specifying patients' wishes should they become unable to make decisions for themselves. The Durable Power of Attorney for Health Care, or a health care proxy, specifies both an individual to speak on your behalf and what treatments you want and those you do not want [regarding a ventilator, CPR, tube feedings, transfusions, etc.] all within a hospital setting. In a home setting, a DNR is a doctor's order prohibiting the use of CPR to emergency responders. Many states today accept a POLST (Physician Orders for Life Sustaining Treatment) which is a doctor's signed order for both home and hospital.

Adult Protective Services (APS) – This is a state program in every county in the country, and APS must investigate any report of suspected abuse.

Advocate – A person who speaks or writes in support of another person.

Alcohol Abuse Disorder (AUD) – Instead of using terms such as alcoholic, and addict, it is now called alcohol use disorder or AUD, and there are new treatment modalities, new thinking, and new medications that make managing AUD more successful than in the past.

Area Agency on Aging (AAA) – A federal program available to help you find helpful resources. There are hundreds of AAAs throughout the country ensuring access to all manner of elder and caregiver assistance and information in most local areas.

Cardiopulmonary Resuscitation (CPR) – An attempt to restart the heart and lungs, which have stopped working. It involves chest compressions, medications, electric shock, and possibly a tube placed in the windpipe for breathing.

Care Manager – Usually a registered nurse or social worker working independently or with a home care agency or elder law attorney. The care manager's job is to set an appointment with the family in the elder's home, do an assessment, establish trust, and develop an individualized plan of care.

Certified Nursing Assistant (CNA) – Someone who has had some training in the field of personal care. They have completed a course of study and have passed an exam attesting to their knowledge of these skills.

Communal Aging Facilities – These are communities of elders who have gathered together to either live in a small enclave, which they have financed, or elders who live in an area and are organized to give help to one another as the need arises.

Continuing Care Retirement Communities (CCRCs) – This is the Cadillac of elder living and care. You may enter as an independent elder and know that you will be taken care of no matter what may happen until your death. These facilities provide independent living, assisted living, and skilled nursing services.

Custodial Care – Non-skilled care such as incontinence care (adult brief changes), bathing, dressing, eating, toileting. This role does not require a college educated professional.

Do Not Resuscitate order (DNR) – This order is for the home setting. If a patient is in a state of decline due to a chronic or terminal illness and anticipates dying at home, a DNR ensures that the emergency medical team will only perform comfort measures and no life saving procedures. This requires a physician's signed order.

Durable Power of Attorney for Healthcare (DPOATHC or Advanced Directives) – This document is for the hospital setting. This is where you are able to state your wishes should you be unable to speak for yourself. Hospitals will ask for a copy of your advanced directives.

Durable Medical Equipment (DME) – Adaptive equipment to remedy deficiencies and barriers of daily life. Can be obtained at a drug store or DME company. A doctor or therapist may also prescribe some DME equipment. Some insurance coverage may be available for these devices. For example: walkers, wheelchairs, shower chairs, hospital beds, canes, nebulizers, catheters, etc.

Durable Power of Attorney for Finances (POA Finance) – Legally allows another person to act on one's behalf. This allows them to sign documents and manage finances.

Geriatrician – Medical doctor specializing in the care of the elderly.

Hospice – End of life care relieving patients of pain and other symptoms managed by a caring team of professionals made up of a physician, registered nurses, social workers, home health aides for personal care, a chaplain, counselors, and volunteers. A physical therapist may be used for safety concerns and equipment issues. Hospice's purpose is to improve the quality of life for the elder and the family. Bereavement services are offered to the family after death occurs.

Independent Transportation Networks (ITN) – A group of non-profits that match seniors with volunteer drivers providing door-to-door service in ITN vans.

Instrumental Activities of Daily Living (IADLs) – A list of home care tasks used to evaluate a person's ability to live independently. These tasks include housekeeping, use of phone, bill paying and managing financial matters, getting groceries, laundry, food preparation, transportation, and taking medication correctly.

Licensed Vocational Nurse (LVN) – A healthcare provider who renders basic nursing care. Care is provided under the direction of a physician or registered nurse.

Long Term Care Insurance – Insurance designed to cover costs for care over an extended period in nursing homes, assisted living facilities, Alzheimer's facilities, and to cover nursing costs in the home. This is insurance that the elder has bought and paid for each month over a period of time, but the elder must qualify before the insurer pays a benefit.

Meals on Wheels (MOW) – This is a program that provides meals to those who are unable to prepare their own, or are homebound.

Medicare – Health insurance provided by the federal government for those over 65 who have worked and paid into the system.

Medicaid – A state and federal health care program for those with limited resources.

Over-the-Counter medication (OTCs) – Medications available for purchase without a prescription, such as Tylenol, aspirin or Benadryl, etc.

Physician Orders for Life Sustaining Treatment (POLST) – This is a legal form recognized in some states that combines advanced directives and the do-not-resuscitate order, covering both home and hospital settings.

Polypharmacy – The use of multiple prescription medications as well as OTCs, vitamins, and supplements by a patient. Concerns about both adverse reactions and interactions of these drugs should be addressed by your physician. By having your PHR with you at every doctor visit, your drug regimen can be evaluated. Do not hesitate to ask your physician if your medication regime can be simplified.

Registered Nurse (RN) – A nurse who has graduated from a nursing program and passed any necessary tests to obtain a nursing license.

Reverse Mortgage – A loan secured by borrowing against the equity of your home. You and your spouse must be sixty-two years or older. In a reverse mortgage, the lender pays you a lump sum or monthly payments based on the equity of your home.

Personal Health Record (PHR) – An up-to-date personal health record that includes the following information: all relevant history, allergies, medications, ailments, medical devices, pharmacy etc. (See Chapter 2 for more information.)

Senior Centers – For a nominal fee, these local centers offer an array of activities and socialization for the elderly.

Skilled Nursing Facility (SNF) – A health care facility meeting Medicare and Medicaid standards for reimbursement. These facilities provide rehabilitation services following hospitalization for surgeries and illnesses plus long-term care.

Special Care Units (SCU) – Either a free-standing facility or designated floors within a larger facility to meet the special needs of people with a specific disease or condition such as Alzheimer's disease.

Trust – A legal document that usually contains a will and is an arrangement for a person to manage assets for another. It limits probate court involvement after death and may provide assets to the client before death.

Will – A legal document that specifies how assets/property will be distributed after one's death. May be included in a trust.

ENDNOTES

PROLOGUE

1. Leo Tolstoy, *A Confession* (Accessible Publishing Systems 2008), 40-41.
2. Judith Viorst, *Necessary Losses* (New York: Simon & Schuster, 1986).
3. Andrew Weil, *Healthy Aging A Lifelong Guide to Your Physical and Spiritual Wellbeing* (New York: Alfred Knopf, 2005).

CHAPTER THREE SAFETY

1. AARP Bulletin article. www.aarp.org/bulletin/
2. The Fall Prevention Center of Excellence. www.stopfalls.org

CHAPTER FOUR MEDICAL CARE AND MEDICATIONS

1. http://todaysgeriatricmedicine.com (new site for Aging Well)
2. http://todaysgeriatricmedicine.com (new site for Aging Well)

CHAPTER FIVE QUALITY OF LIFE

1. Centenarian Study. www.bumc.bu.edu/centenarian/overview/
2. www.aarp.org
3. www.elderlink.org
4. www.eldercarelink.com/Nursing Homes/Investigating-the-Culture-Change-in Nursing-Home-Care.htm
5. Ibid.
6. *Genworth 2014 Cost of Care Survey.* https://www.genworth.com/dam/Americas/US/PDFs/Consumer/corporate/130568_032514_CostofCare_FINAL_nonsecure.pdf

CHAPTER SIX SOCIALIZATION

1. http://www.ncoa.org/press-room/fact-sheets/senior-centers-fact-sheet.html

CHAPTER SEVEN NUTRITION

1. www.mowaa.org
2. http://www.uptodate.com/contents/approach-to-the-patient-with-weight-loss
3. www.personalchef.com
4. Michael Pollan, *The Omnivore's Dilemma: A Natural History of Four Meals* (New York: Penguin, 2006).
5. www.newteethforme.com/denture-solutions

CHAPTER EIGHT DRIVING

1. Insurance Institute for Highway Safety. www.iihs.org
2. www.nhmagazine.com/June-2013/Elderly-Drivers-and-Safety-in-New-Hampshire
3. www.slate.com/articles/life/family/2012/03/when_to_stop_driving_why_it_is_so_hard_to_get_elderly_drivers_off_the_road_.1.html
4. www.iihs.org
5. http://www.aarp.org/home-garden/transportation/we_need_to_talk/?intcmp=DSO-SEARCH-AARPSUGG
6. http://www.aota.org/en/About-Occupational-Therapy/Professionals/PA/Articles/Driving.aspx

CHAPTER NINE ALCOHOL AND DRUG ABUSE

1. Aging Well, summer 2008.
2. www.niaa.nih.gov/alcohol-health/special-populations-co-occurring-disorders/older-adults
3. http://www.psychweekly.com/aspx/article/ArticleDetail.aspx?articleid=19
4. http://www.aafp.org/afp/2000/0315/p1710.html
5. www.nihseniorhealth.gov/alcoholuse/howalcoholaffectssafety/01.html
6. www.nihseniorhealth.gov/alcoholabuse/alcoholand aging/01.html
7. www.niaaa.nih.gov/alcohol-health/special-populations-co-occurring-disorders/older-adults
8. www.nihseniorhealth.gov/alcoholuse/ifyoudrink/0.1html
9. www.nia.nih.gov/health/publication/alcohol-use-older-people

10. Role of family members (Alcoholism in the Elderly March 15, 2000 American Academy of Family Physicians).

CHAPTER TEN Dementia Symptoms and Alzheimer's Disease

1. A Dementia Fact Sheet published September 22, 2009. www.knowingmore.com
2. Dr. Jerome Groopman, MD, Why Doctors Make Mistakes, article in AARP Magazine, September/October 2008.
3. A Dementia Fact Sheet published September 22, 2009. www.knowingmore.com
4. Alzheimer's association Stages of Alzheimer's. www.alz.org/alzheimers_disease_stages_of_alzheimers.asp
5. Caregiver Kit, Support for Those Who Care for Others. Northwest Regional Council/Area Agency on Aging. Family Caregiver Support Project.
6. Advice for Family Caregivers from other Caregivers: Snohomish County Long Term Care and Aging.
7. www.alz.org/care/alzheimers-dementtia-gps-comfortzone.asp
8. ABCs for the Care of People with Dementia, Santa Cruz Alzheimer's Association. 831-464-9982.
9. http://www.alz.org/care/alzheimers-dementia-adult-day-centers. aspwww.alz.org/carefinder
10. http://www.alz.org/care/alzheimers-dementia-common-costs.asp
11. Ibid.
12. Ibid.

CHAPTER ELEVEN Elder Abuse and Scams

1. www.socialpc.com/Socialissues/Scams-on-the-Elderly.html
2. http://www.doh.wa.gov/portals/1/Documents/ Pubs/669256-W09.pdf
3. http://www.statisticbrain.com/elderly-abuse-statistics/
4. http://www.aoa.gov/AoARoot/AoA_Programs/Elder_Rights/Elder_Abuse/Index.aspx
5. http://www.aarp.org/money/scams-fraud/info-03-2013/ skip-humphreys-mission-protection.2.html
6. Ibid.
7. http://www.aoa.gov/AoA_programs/Elder_Rights/EA_Prevention/WhatToDo.aspx

8. Ibid.
9. www.preventelderabuse.org/elderabuse/issues/substance.html
10. http://www.ncoa.org/enhance-economic-security/economic-secu-rity-Initiative/savvy-saving-seniors/top-10-scams-targeting.html
11. www.fraud.org/tips/telemarketing/avoid.html

CHAPTER TWELVE Death and Grief

1. Mark Frost, *The Match: The Day the Game of Golf Changed Forever* (New York: Good Comma Ink, Inc. 2007).
2. Felix Carrion, Stillspeaking Devotional. Dailydevotional@ucc.org
3. http://www.brainyquote.com/quotes/authors/e/elisabeth_kubler-ross.html
4. Gawande, Atul, *Being Mortal*, (Canada: Doubleday Canada, 2014).
5. Barbara Karnes, *Gone From My Sight, The Dying Experience.* 1986.
6. Barbara Kate Repa, What is a Green Funeral? November 7, 2012. www.caring.com/questions/what-is-a-green-funeral?
7. www.helpguide.org
8. Kate Maloy, *Every Last Cuckoo* (Algonquin Books of Chapel Hill, NC, 2008).
9. George Eliott, *Middlemarch*, (New York: Penguin Classics 1994. First published 1871).
10. Dr. William Sloan, When Time Doesn't Heal All Wounds, article in Medinfo, Northwest Hospital and Medical Center, UW Medicine January-February 2011.
11. Grief workshop given by Carol Scott Kassner at the University Congregational United Church of Christ, Seattle, WA. 2011.
12. https://www.americanhospice.org/grief/working-through-grief/85-helping-your-bereaved-friend
13. Henry Scott Holland, (January 27, 1847 to March 17, 1918) was Regius Professor of Divinity at the University of Oxford. http://www.poeticexpressions.co.uk/POEMS/Death%20is%20nothing%20at%20all%20-%20Canon%20Henry%20Scott-Holland.htm

EPILOGUE

1. https://www.ted.com/speakers/dan_buettner

BIBLIOGRAPHY

BOOKS

Bell, Virginia & Troxel, David. *The Best Friends Approach to Alzheimer's Care*. Baltimore, Maryland: Health Professions Press, Inc. 3rd printing, 2009.

Clendinen, Dudley. *A Place Called Canterbury, Tales of the New Old Age in America*. New York, NY: Penguin Group 2008.
(I love this book! It gives a wonderful picture of aging in a facility and is filled with humor as well as pathos about those aging in community.)

Eliott, George. *Middlemarch*. New York: Penguin Classics, 1994.

Ellis, Neenah. *If I Live to be 100. Lessons From the Centenarians*. New York: Three Rivers Press, 2004.
(These stories were originally broadcast on NPR, and are now compiled into book form. They are inspiring and informative of lives well-lived into old age.)

Gawande, Atul. *Being Mortal: Medicine and What Matters in the End*. Canada: Doubleday Canada, 2014.
(This book touches my core because it stated with eloquence and compassion what I have been struggling with for decades. How can medicine, as it is presently practiced, enhance the best quality of life toward the end of our lives? Don't miss reading this book!)

Heilbrun, Carolyn B. *The Last Gift of Time, Life Beyond Sixty*. New York: Ballantine Publishing Group 1997.
(This is a story of a woman who did not want to grow old, and she planned to exit life on her own terms. She then found that aging was some of the best times of her life.)

Karnes, Barbara. *Gone From My Sight, The Dying Experience*. Barbara Karnes Books, 1986.
(This small handbook is one of the most informative books for families facing the imminent death of a loved one. It is easy to read and understand as well as comforting.)

Kehl, Richard. *It Takes a Long Time to Become Young, Words to Grow Young By*. Blue Laughing Studio, 2008.
(The chapter quotes came from this book.)

Mace, Nancy and Rabins, Peter MD. *The 36 Hour Day, A Family Guide to Caring for People Who have Alzheimer's Disease, Related Dementias, and Memory Loss.* Baltimore, Md: Johns Hopkins University Press 1981.
(This landmark book is over 30 years old and is still one of the best sources of information about Alzheimer's disease. Its latest printing and update is 2012.)

Maloy, Kate. *Every Last Cuckoo.* Chapel Hill NC: Algonquin Books, 2008.
(This novel is a poignant and well written novel of a woman who loses her husband and soul mate. It is how she copes and recovers along with her adult children. It is a favorite of mine.)

Martz, Sandra Haldeman. *If I Had My Life to Live Over I Would Pick More Daisies.* Watsonville, CA: Paper-Mache Press, 1992.
(This is an anthology of wonderful poems and stories about aging. I keep referring to it for inspiration.)

Pollan, Michael. *The Omnivore's Dilemma: A Natural History of Four Meals.* New York: Penguin, 2006.
(This fascinating book tells of the new science around nutrition and explains in very simple terms how we should be eating to nourish our bodies into old age.)

Spohr, Betty Baker. *To Hold a Falling Star, A Personal Story of Living at Home with Alzheimer's.* Stanford, CT: Longmeadow Press 1990.
(This is one of my favorite books on Alzheimer's disease. It is very readable, short, and filled with practical information that allowed this woman to care for her husband at home.)

Tolstoy, Leo. *A Confession.* Accessible Publishing Systems 2008.
(Tolstoy tells us of his struggles to live an integral life knowing that all lives eventually end.)

Viorst, Judith. *Necessary Losses.* New York: Simon and Schuster 1986.
(I read this book as a young woman and have reread it several times as I have aged. It deals with losses at every stage of our life, thus preparing us for the losses involved with growing old.)

Weil, Andrew. *Healthy Aging: A Lifelong Guide to Your Physical and Spiritual Wellbeing.* New York: Alfred Knopf, 2005.
(This very positive and informative book, like the man who wrote it, leads us into our aging journey with sage advice on not only our physical wellbeing but also our spiritual wellbeing.)

WEBSITES

Administration for Community Living
www.acl.gov

American Academy of Family Physicians
www.aafp.org

American Association of Retired People
www.aarp.org/money/scams-fraud/
www.aarp.org/bulletin
www.aarp.org/home-garden/transportation/we_need_to_talk/

Alzheimer's Association (for information on daycare centers, common
costs, GPS, etc.)
www.alz.org

American Hospice Foundation (a good section on grief)
www.americanhospice.org

Administration on Aging
www.aoa.gov

American Occupational Therapist Association (for elder driving
abilities)
www.aota.org

Barbara Karnes, RN, hospice educator, author of *Gone From My Sight*
bkbooks.com

New England Centenarian Study from Boston University School of
Medicine
www.bumc.bu.edu/centenarian/overview

Caring.Com (helping caregivers find support and resources; green
funerals)
www.caring.com

Elder care (resource for finding services for elders)
www.eldercarelink.com

National Consumers League (help in combating scams)
www.fraud.org

Genworth Insurance (2014 cost of care survey has info from every
state regarding prices for long term care)
www.genworth.com

Healthcare Professional Network
www.hcplive.com

Resolving health challenges for elders
www.helpguide.org

Insurance Institute for Highway Safety (see Topics/Older drivers)
www.iihs.org

For elder transportation needs
www.itnamerica.org
www.seniorsservices.org/transportation/hydeshuttles.aspx

Meals on Wheels
www.mowaa.org

Adult Protective Services
www.napsa-now.org

American Health Information Management Association to create your
own Personal Health Record [PDR]
www.myphr.com

National adult Day Services association (For info on adult day care)
www.nadsa.org

National Center on Elder Abuse
www.ncea.aoa.gov

National Council on Aging
www.ncoa.org

denture solutions
www.newteethforme.com

For info on smoke alarms and fire safety
www.nfpa.org/safety-information/

New Hampshire Magazine ("Elder Drivers and Safety in New
Hampshire" by Leeann Doherty)
www.nhmagazine.com/June-2013

National Institute on Aging (article on alcohol use in elders)
www.nia.nih.gov/health/publication/alcohol-use-older-people

National Institute of Alcohol Abuse and Alcoholism (search: Older
Adults)
www.niaaa.nih.gov

National Association of Area Agencies on Aging (the umbrella agency in Washington, D.C. representing all the Area Agencies on Aging in the country)
www.n4a.org

Durable Power of Attorney for Finances, (for the forms you'll need)
www.nolo.com
www.lawdepot.com
www.rocketlawyer.com

American Personal & Private Chef Association (to find and hire a personal chef)
www.personalchef.com

Physician Orders for Life-Sustaining Treatment paradigm
www.polst.org

National Committee for the Prevention of Elder Abuse
www.preventelderabuse.org

Social PC (search: Social Issues/Scams On the Elderly)
www.socialpc.com

Fall Prevention Center of Excellence
www.stopfalls.org

Teepa Snow (an occupational therapist specializing in dementia, lots of good information)
www.teepasnow.com

Today's Geriatric Medicine (for those working with elders)
www.todaysgeriatricmedicine.com

Up To Date (latest health information for medical professionals)
www.uptodate.com/contents/approach-to-the-patient-with-weight-loss

INDEX

ACKNOWLEDGMENTS

We always stand on the shoulders of others when we attempt to write a book or accomplish similar arduous adventures. Professionally, I am indebted to several people who mentored me along the way regarding all forms of elder care. Early in my career, Carol Snow, MSN, RN, administrator of the Visiting Nurse Association in Monterey, CA, took a chance on hiring me and then carefully taught me all the intricacies of Medicare home care. John O'Brien, CEO and owner of Central Coast Senior Services in Pacific Grove, CA, is a compassionate champion of elders and a mentor extraordinaire. He taught me volumes about the care management of elders in the private sector. We only grow when those who walk before us turn back and spend time, talent, and treasure helping those behind them. I am also grateful to Susan "Sam" Miller, RN, MN, ARNP, and Diedrich Meinken, MSW, co-owners of Care Force, an elder care management and home care company in Lynnwood, WA, for giving me a wonderful, nurturing environment to finish out my career before retiring.

I owe a huge debt of gratitude to my lifelong friend, Anne Petrovich, PhD, Professor Emeritus at Fresno State University in the Department of Social Work. Anne provided invaluable wisdom throughout this process, giving me excellent feedback and insights on the content of the book. I am forever in her debt.

Without the love and support of my family, this book would not have been written. My two children, Jennifer and Andrew, were enthusiastic from the very conception of the idea. Their two partners, Tim and Anka, have also been avid enthusiasts and coaches. My deep appreciation to Tim for introducing me to John Budz and Vee Sawyer of Ward Street Press. John and Vee believed in this book from the very beginning and provided exceptional guidance, honest critique, and artful design to bring it to life.

Last, but far from least, is my deep gratitude to the countless elders and their families who invited me into their homes at vulnerable and tender times in their lives. They taught me the art of traversing this *Journey through Old*.

ABOUT THE AUTHOR

Susan received her BS in Nursing from the University of Rochester, New York, and has been a Registered Nurse for over forty years. She spent the first part of her career in pediatrics and mission nursing in Egypt and West Africa. She then moved into elder care, as well as care management, which has become her specialty over the past twenty years. She has deep experience in both the Medicare home care industry and the private care arena. Susan lives in Seattle, Washington, near both of her children and their families.

Susan Towle's professional experiences inspired her to write *Old Is Not a Four-Letter Word*. She hopes to transform people's perception of aging from dread and denial into a journey of preparation and a willingness to embrace aging as a precious gift.

■ ■ ■

COLOPHON

The main text for
Old Is Not a Four-Letter Word
is set in Adobe Garamond Pro. A beautiful
old-style face, based on the original cutouts Claude
Garamont created in the early Sixteenth Century. Today
in its digital form Adobe Garamond remains a large
clear face and its flow in blocks of type make
it eminently readable and friendly for
the *Journey through Old*.